YAHOO INCOME

How Anyone of Any Age, Location, and/or Background Can Build a Highly Profitable Online Business With Yahoo

by Dana E. Blozis
and Sharon L. Cohen

Yahoo Income: How Anyone of Any Age, Location, and/or Background Can Build a Highly Profitable Online Business With Yahoo

ISBN-13: 978-1-60138-254-2

Library of Congress Cataloging-in-Publication Data
Blozis, Dana E., 1967-
 Yahoo income : how anyone of any age, location, and/or background can build a highly profitable online business with Yahoo / by Dana E. Blozis and Sharon L. Cohen.
     p. cm.
 Includes bibliographical references and index.
 ISBN-13: 978-1-60138-254-2 (alk. paper)
 ISBN-10: 1-60138-254-5 (alk. paper)
 1. Yahoo! Inc. 2. Electronic commerce. 3. Business enterprises--Computer networks. I. Cohen, Sharon, 1949- II. Title.
 HF5548.32.B597 2009
 658.8'72--dc22
                                        2009015120

COVER DESIGN: Meg Buchner • megadesn@mchsi.com
Printed in the United States

Contents

CHAPTER 3
Are You Ready to Yahoo!? — 43

CHAPTER 4
Getting Started: Business Basics, Part 1 — 65

CHAPTER 5
Getting Started: Business Basics, Part 2 — 81

CHAPTER 6
Choosing Your Yahoo! Plan Level   93

CHAPTER 7
Yahoo! Tools and Services   103

CHAPTER 10
Control Panels for Easy-to-Make
Store Changes   163

CHAPTER 11
Running Your Yahoo! Store   189

CHAPTER 12
Marketing Your Yahoo! Store, Part 1   215

CHAPTER 13
Marketing Your Yahoo! Store, Part 2   225

CHAPTER 14
Marketing Your Yahoo! Store, Part 3   249

Yahoo! Just Keeps Going   299

List of Yahoo Services   307

Bibliography   312

CHAPTER 1

Introduction to Yahoo!

Yahoo! – A Slice of Online History

From its humble beginnings in 1994 as "Jerry and David's Guide to the World Wide Web," international Web portal Yahoo! has exploded in popularity, now serving more than 345 million users every month.

Founded by Stanford doctoral students Jerry Yang and David Filo, the site originally began as a personal listing of Internet sites the men visited frequently. As the list grew into the hundreds, it became difficult to manage, so Yang and Filo organized the information into categories, and eventually subcategories, essentially creating a primitive online directory.

Word of the project spread to their friends and other users, propelling the directory from homegrown status to an international Web portal offering countless resources and services to users around the world. The following fall, the site celebrated its first million-hit day.

According to the Yahoo! Web site, Yang and Filo recognized the business potential of the newly renamed Yahoo!, an acronym for "Yet Another Hierarchical Officious Oracle," and incorporated in

March of 1995. The following month, the pair received an initial investment of $2 million from a group of venture capitalists from Silicon Valley. Additional funding was secured in the fall of 1995, followed by a successful initial public offering (NASDAQ: YHOO) in April of 1996.

Yahoo! Now

Thirteen years later, Yahoo! is more than just a search engine. Its Web site reports that it has evolved into an online giant, serving more than 500 million unique visitors in 20 different languages. Based in Sunnyvale, California, Yahoo! employs 12,000 staff members and serves more than 20 different global markets, including Europe, Asia Pacific, Latin America, Canada, and the United States.

Why Yahoo!?

Ask both new and long-term Yahoo! merchants why they chose Yahoo! as their online business platform over many other competitors, some as well-known as Amazon, and you will hear numerous positive comments about the Yahoo! brand's easy-to-use yet robust Web site and excellent customer service. As you will see in the case studies, developers and store owners alike say that Yahoo! is the best option for starting a new home business or growing an existing one. Better yet, over the years, thousands of small and large e-commerce owners continue to successfully use Yahoo's! Web site store platform to build highly profitable business ventures. In fact, in 2008 *PC Magazine* gave an Editors' Choice award to Yahoo! Merchant Solutions. The editors noted that Yahoo! SiteBuilder is a Web site program that gives thousands of merchants the power to construct their site from scratch or from their available templates.

Yahoo! has built in a non-vanilla look to its merchant sites. Not only are the Web sites able to be tailored to the sellers' needs, but the Yahoo! software actually offers customizable, highly professional templates for e-commerce owners to use. The Yahoo! SiteBuilder system also gives sellers the ability to use specific positioning in addition to drag-and-drop editing and layering and FTP uploading capabilities. It is also possible to add royalty-free graphics and use e-commerce functionality and clip art. The SiteBuilder application can be run from the merchant's desktop while they are designing their own Web site offline. In addition, the Yahoo! platform allows multimedia content and embedding of audio and video files directly into the Web pages.

Yahoo! does not leave anyone in the lurch, not even newbies who never put up a Web site. The customer service team is right there for their customers, just like they should be. Plus, there is a 530-plus page manual that goes over everything, step by step, to help build the site.

Yahoo! Merchant Solutions provides all Internet sellers, from Internet newbies to million-dollar businesses, everything they need to build, host, manage, expand, and promote their online store. For what many developers charge thousands of dollars, Yahoo! starts at about $40 or less, if you are new and just want to establish your presence online. Sherry Comes from Coffeecake.com calls this "one of the best-kept secrets."

Although someone who has little or no experience in building an online store can create, manage, and maintain Yahoo! Merchant Solutions' online tools, such as Store Manager, Catalog Manager, and Store Editor, it is also always possible to add on numerous advanced store features as needed that may require external Web site development expertise. These services include constructing complex Web site templates; integrating your store with external back-office applications, with CGI scripts and XML; or providing product lists to external shopping engines. Yahoo! even recommends a list of highly qualified developers to provide these extra services for reasonable costs.

One of the strong points of going with Yahoo! Merchant Solutions is that you are not just buying a Web site, but rather, a full "solution" for your business. Therefore, Yahoo! is not just there to help you put up your Web site, but to give you the tools and techniques, as well as the input of other Yahoo! merchants. Yahoo!'s Small Business resource site and library includes a host of articles that cover everything from writing a business plan and determining a domain name to employment law and shipping suggestions. There are also videos of successful Yahoo! store owners who provide some of their tips and best practices on how to grow a business. You can also view the tutorials on such subjects as sponsored search and analytics and attend webinars about topics such as creating special campaigns and pricing. Rather than starting from scratch, it is best to see what does or does not work with others and then adapt it to your own needs.

When Jerry Yang and David Filo decided to call their tiny Web site Yahoo!, it is doubtful they realized how the name would become so well known around the world. This unique name helped build the company's branding and positive image as an approachable place for a fun Internet experience and a friendly place to do business. Over the years, it has become a strong brand that has helped Yahoo Inc. to continue its growth, despite the ups and downs of the industry and competition and takeover tries from rivals, such as Google and Microsoft. For Yahoo! merchants, the most important aspect of this branding is the fact that the name is not only well known, but also perceived as a safe, reliable place to do business.

A Web site that says "powered by Yahoo!" is backed by millions of dollars of advertising and marketing dollars that continue to make the brand name strong throughout the world. Where other sites, such as Google, do not stick to their brand name when adding services (Gmail, for example), Yahoo! proudly slaps its name on nearly everything it produces, from Yahoo! Mail, Yahoo! Shopping, and Yahoo! Autos, to Yahoo! Merchant Solutions. It interconnects its various services with links throughout its sites, which draws customers into your Web business from many different portals.

With your monthly low-cost fee, you get several tools to help get your new business going. Yet, as you want to grow, additional marketing and advertising will be important. Once again, this could be costly if you did not have the support and strength of a company like Yahoo! behind you. Yahoo!, for example, offers easy, affordable ways for display advertising, where you can create your own ad without the expense of a designer or developer, build a campaign for your target audience, and even track daily performance against desired goals. Perhaps even more important, the ads will be seen. Every day, 47 million people use Yahoo!, and users conduct 2.4 billion searches every month.

Yahoo! is regularly improving its small business services. Geo-targeting enhancements help you pinpoint your target customers. Knowing that your advertisements will show up for the right people in the right locations is critical, particularly when your business specifically caters to a niche audience. Geo-targeting gives you the opportunity to tailor your targeting strategies, whether you want to reach the whole country or just zoom in on a city or ZIP code. Geo-targeting analyzes search queries, Internet Protocol (IP) addresses, and similar information to determine where a user is located and what ads to serve to that user. For example, if you select Boston as a geo-targeted region for the sale of your product, users with an IP address in Boston will be served your ad. If you are a Boston-based business, you likely will get more relevant traffic, which can lead to more sales.

The case studies demonstrate that Yahoo! merchants also greatly appreciate another recent addition to their marketing efforts: the analytic tool that allows Web sites to track metrics on their customers' online behavior. One of the key benefits of the analytics is real-time reports. If you have someone come to your Web site at 8:04 a.m., at 8:05 a.m., you can see what that person did after arrival. Watching such behavior can have a major impact on conversion rates, since you can see why a person does not buy everything put into his or her shopping cart. If only 2 percent of people are converted, how come the other 98 percent are not?

CASE STUDY: CHIP BULKELEY

Chip Bulkeley, Owner
CHiP's V6 Specialties
P.O. Box 151035
Fort Worth, Texas 76108
817-726-2781
http://www.chipsv6specialties.com

Chip Bulkeley, owner of CHiPs V6 Specialties, has used the power of Yahoo! Merchant Solutions to increase the sales power of his business. In 2003 Chip and Linda Bulkeley were spending "tons of time" searching the Internet for information on how to fix up their 1997-3.8L V6 Ford Mustang. His father wisely asked, "Did you ever think about setting up your own Web site for Mustang V6 and GT enthusiasts?" After initially thinking, "You got to be kidding!" Chip Bulkeley saw the wisdom in this question. "We wanted a site that would cater to the beginner and beyond."

He started looking around for a way to start his new Web site and balked at the prices of $10,000 to $15,000 from designers. Then he read about Yahoo! and decided the $39.95 monthly Internet service provider fee to build the site was much easier to digest! With the help of the 384-page Web-site Getting Started guide and the 24/7 customer service team, "little by little," he says, "I grew my site. There never was a time when someone in customer service didn't help me."

In 2006 at the request of his visitors, he began adding V6 Mustang performance products and upgrade kits to his Web site. He now has agreements with five wholesalers and still finds it quite easy to add and change his product listings.

CASE STUDY: CHIP BULKELEY

He's pleased to see that Yahoo! is improving its search functions with the Store Manager function, which has been a problem. Also, when Yahoo! signed an agreement with PayPal for the shopping cart, Bulkeley's sales went up 35 percent.

Bulkeley is glad that he went to Yahoo!, not only because of the price and ease of use, but also because of the brand name. He knows that the Yahoo! Secure Buyer Protection statement on his site shows that he is a reputable merchant. He also knows that Yahoo! keeps its quality levels high: "If you prove yourself less than aboveboard, Yahoo! kicks you out," he explains. Anyone who understands the high-quality and performance of the Mustang V6 knows that his Web site has to convey that same quality.

Yahoo!'s analytic's tool provides information that the majority of stores do not have at their fingertips. Yahoo! owners use this tool to decrease the number of dropped carts, lower the bounce rates to other pages, see why customers leave the site, determine whether ads are in the right position, and look at particular niche usage of the site. Owners can watch the movement of a customer from search engine, to landing page, to product page, and then to the check out or exit. In other words, the Web sites can see what they are and are not doing right. Analytics is a powerful tool for increasing sales and monthly income.

Similarly, the "checkout page cross-sell" tool tells your customer about other products you sell that are similar to the ones being purchased, and thus increases your value order per order. Customers can find similar products and get discounts for purchasing any cross-sell items to which they are alerted. It can increase your average sale and help your customers readily add products directly from the shopping cart. Benefits include: selling accessories with the main item; increasing the order value per order; showing item-specific or storewide cross-sells; increasing the average size of each order; providing merchants with an easy-to-use, easy-to-update process; keeping customers on the specific-product page, decreasing customer time needed to purchase cross-sell products and enhancing customer satisfaction.

The Internet presents endless opportunities for retailers of all types, and merchants have a host of companies that want to sell them Web sites. Yet, in order for netpreneurs to maximize their online results and be economically successful in a business, it is essential that they have the advantages of a well-framed online store. Yahoo! store development can be the perfect solution to all the complexities associated with virtual stores. The design is an excellent opportunity for newly launched online stores that want to continue their growth. It presents e-commerce Web site design in a way that has the capability of engaging target customers, holding their attention, and encouraging them to make a sale and then come back for more.

ere is a quick review of the reasons why you should seriously consider using Yahoo! as your online store:

- The Yahoo! brand is recognized and respected throughout the world. Shoppers feel safe with Yahoo!, which means they will feel safe ordering your products.

- By using the Yahoo! name on your Web site, you are benefiting from all of Yahoo!'s marketing and promotion.

- Yahoo! can be considered a grandfather of the Internet. It was one of the first major online entities and has grown ever since.

- Customer service ranks on the top of Yahoo!'s list. Not only does the company care about the customers who buy its products, it also cares about the success of its merchants. The customer care center is open 24/7 to help with your needs.

- The Yahoo! store is known for its ease of use and flexibility. It is just as effective for a person starting up in the business as it is for someone who has thousands of products to sell. It expands as you expand your E-commerce venture.

- It is unlikely that you could you get a Web site, support, and marketing anywhere else for such a low fee.

- Yahoo! is continually adding new, state-of-the art technology, such as its analytics tool.

- Placement of your products on Yahoo! Shopping.

- Discounts, coupons, or special promotions and products featured on both Yahoo! and Google search engines.

- Cross-promotion or products at customer checkout.

- Return on investment (ROI) for high-traffic marketing.

No one who has opened a successful store online will say that it is easy. It takes a great deal of time, commitment, and effort regardless of what platform you use. Now, with greater competition than ever, it takes someone who has found the right business niche and is willing to do whatever it takes to promote it. However, when you begin your venture with a name like Yahoo!, it is like you have a strong head start. There are thousands of new netpreneurs who are successfully using Yahoo!, in addition to several well-known names, including Lance Armstrong Foundation and its Livestrong® Store and Ben&Jerry's Ice cream by Mail.

Yahoo! Merchant Solutions

It would take years and many books to write about everything Yahoo! has to offer in the online marketplace and beyond. To make it easier, we will narrow our focus to Yahoo! Merchant Solutions. We will show you how to leverage this opportunity to your benefit, so you can own one of the 72,000 Yahoo! shops online today.

As will be described in greater detail in the following chapters, Yahoo! Merchant Solutions offers online store owners three different packages, depending on the level of services you would like to receive. Upgrading plans is extremely easy, so you can always upgrade later as your business grows.

REAL-TIME STRENGTH OF YAHOO!

According to many of the Yahoo! storeowners and developers, one of the big advantages of Yahoo! Merchant Solutions Web site development is its unique use of RTML (Real Time Markup Language), a powerful, yet flexible programming language.

REAL-TIME STRENGTH OF YAHOO!

The history of RTML stems back to 1995, the earliest days of the World Wide Web. Paul Graham and Robert Morris created a company called ViaWeb, using their proprietary language, RTML. It not only was useful for making Web sites, but was extremely search engine friendly.

In 1998, Yahoo! acquired ViaWeb because RTML was believed to be a perfect fit for the already successful Yahoo! stores. It allowed Yahoo! the opportunity to offer merchants complete setup, design, hosting, and promotional services for their e-commerce stores. Best of all, it was the first Web site authoring tool and hosting service that provided nontechnical users the ability to instantly create, publish and manage high-quality, secure online stores.

Here are some of its benefits:

- You can determine the structure of the entire Web site, not only the material on the separate pages.

- With only a few lines, you can create images as well as text.

- RTML offers predefined variations of commonly needed CGI-scripts

- Like HTML, if you make an error in a template, there may be a page that looks odd, but an error message does not come up.

- When people program pages for the first time, they are likely to have syntax errors. With RTML, you do not have to type in the whole program, but just choose menu codes and fill in the blanks.

REAL-TIME STRENGTH OF YAHOO!

- No matter what is expressed in RTML can be seen with a typical browser.

- RTML is ready and waiting for the search-engines.

Since RTML was created, scores of other programming systems have been developed for Web stores, including osCommerce, Shopsite, XCart, Amazon, and Ebay Stores. Yet Yahoo's RTML makes it possible for users without knowledge of programming or third-party software to develop Web pages that can economically be highly customized.

E-Commerce for 2009 and Beyond

It is amazing to see how quickly e-commerce developed and grew into the megalith it is today. Further, as anyone who is involved with the Internet knows firsthand, constant change is the only consistency with e-commerce. Just as store owners, online marketers and Web site developers center on one best way to inform and promote, another way emerges, and the earlier one begins to lose its appeal. Recently, for example, blogs and social networks are all the rage. They go hand in hand with very sophisticated, continually refined search engine optimization (SEO) techniques. Yet there are some e-commerce fundamentals that we will cover here, along with a brief acknowledgement of Yahoos!' provision of these basics.

Getting its start in 1996, but stemming back into the 1960s, e-commerce can be defined as "the buying and selling of goods and services on the Internet." It is a relatively new way to sell products and services. As will also be seen in this book, e-commerce has

23

evolved into other areas, such as affiliates, which can be just as lucrative as owning one's own store.

Book Overview

Whether you want to start your own full-time business or just dabble in a side business part-time, this book will show you how to get started. We will take you step by step through the process, explaining everything from naming your business and creating a business plan to creating your online storefront and managing your store. Once you have your store up and running, we will show you how to use Yahoo! services to advertise and market your business, and so much more.

Here is a preview, starting with the next chapter:

Chapter 2: Yahoo! Small Business Overview

Check here for a brief look at the many Yahoo! services and tools you will use as a Yahoo! store merchant. Each of these will be covered in greater depth later in the book.

Chapter 3: Are You Ready to Take the Plunge?

Yahoo! offers many opportunities, and thousands of people have found it a valuable part-time or full time investment or business. That does not mean this type of business, or any business of your own, is right for you. This will give you more information to make this important decision. We will discuss the characteristics, skills, and background you need to own a small business. Use our checklists to find out whether you are ready to take the plunge into self-employment, part time or full time.

Chapter 4: Getting Started, Business Basics, Part 1

Whether your plan is to open one Yahoo! store or twenty, this chapter will tell you how to start your business, beginning with establishing a name and concluding with developing business and marketing plans to set your success in motion.

Chapter 5: Getting Started, Business Basics, Part 2

Now it is time to think about your Mission and Vision and how you will promote these to the outside world. Here are the basics of establishing a marketing plan.

Chapter 6: Choosing Your Yahoo! Plan Level

Depending on your business needs and the size or intended size of your e-commerce store, Yahoo! will give you the support you require.

Chapter 7: Yahoo! Tools and Services

Here, we will get into more depth on each of the Yahoo! tools. You will carefully go through each step to manage your business.

Chapter 8: Put Up Your Storefront, Part 1

We will explain how to create your Yahoo! storefront. We will show you how to use Yahoo!'s tools to set up your store, design it, and publish it to the Web.

Chapter 9: Put Up Your Storefront, Part 2

Now that your Web site is designed, it is time to add the products and catalog copy. You also need to set up a few more business items before you announce your store to the world.

Chapter 10: Control Panels for Easy-to-Make Changes

We have been talking about the front end of your business. Now it is time to get more involved in the back end, where you will be conducting most of your work from now on.

Chapter 11: Running Your Yahoo! Store

With your store open for business, we will offer advice on how to announce your business and draw traffic in using Yahoo! services, and we will give you detailed information about the activities involved in the day-to-day operations of your business.

Chapter 12: Marketing Your Yahoo! Store, Part 1

It is not enough to announce the launch of your Yahoo! store. You must market it regularly, both online and off. In this chapter, we will cover marketing basics using Yahoo!'s online tools.

Chapter 13: Marketing Your Yahoo! Store, Part 2

As described earlier in this book, Yahoo! has numerous products and services to offer Web visitors. We will go through those services and provide you with ideas on how to use them to your advantage to promote and grow your small business.

Chapter 14: Marketing Your Yahoo! Store, Part 3

Here are some of the latest offerings that you can add to your money-making list and instructions on how to write up your overall marketing plan.

Chapter 15: Yahoo! Keeps on Going On

There is always something new and different and Yahoo!

Appendix

As we wrap things up, we include a glossary, worksheets, check-lists, and sample documents for you to use in starting, managing, and promoting your Yahoo! Store.

CHAPTER 2

Yahoo! Small Business Overview

E-commerce is comprised of four primary elements, all of which are needed for a merchant to set up an online store. It must always be kept in mind that the online user is becoming increasingly sophisticated and demanding. When e-commerce first began, and it was still a novelty, consumers were more than willing to put up with glitches, slow or inefficient processes, and errors. This is no longer the case. They want tested, mature processes that will work quickly, effectively, and safely. For you to be successful at your business, it is important that you offer top quality in these four basic areas:

1. An **online catalog of goods and services** where shoppers can review items for sale

2. A **shopping cart** where shoppers can hold items for purchase

3. A **payment gateway** so shoppers can make electronic online payments to sellers

4. An **order processing system** where sellers can process and ship orders to shoppers

No matter what type of business you choose to start, you will need to keep these elements in mind and to choose your vendor carefully. They may look alike, offer similar services, and be priced competitively, but they are not all as simple to use and easy to understand as Yahoo! We will focus our discussion on Yahoo!'s e-commerce offerings.

Online Catalog of Goods and Services

An e-commerce site is similar to a mail-order business, with a list or catalog of goods or services for customers to review and potentially purchase. The success of your e-commerce Web site is based heavily on the quality of your product catalog. Although the product catalog may be the most important aspect of an online store, merchants often overlook it when defining their site. With Yahoo!, you have an easy-to-use system of uploading and managing your products, which will show on your own Web site and on Yahoo! Shopper as well.

The Yahoo! Catalog Manager helps merchants easily manage inventory and organize their merchandise in an online product catalog. They can create a product database, upload or edit items, arrange them by category, and keep track of quantities, all without any need for changing the site's layout or the design of the Web pages. As soon as the Catalog Manager is set up, the store owner can also create "store tags" to integrate product information into the page layout. Then, through the Catalog Manager, the merchant can track inventory, expand offerings, and keep product information up to date. As will be explained in more detail in a later chapter, the catalog configuration and descriptions are crucial to getting visitors to the site, retaining them once they arrive, and encouraging them to actually purchase items they put into their shopping cart and then return to the Web site as needed in the future.

Shopping Cart

When customers visit your e-commerce Web site, they want to be able to find items easily through your catalog system. Then, when it is time for them to check out and purchase their items, they want to do so with ease. Appropriate shopping cart software is designed effectively to tie the customer and payment process together.

How the products look on the Web site when the customers make their decision and put them into their virtual shopping cart is important. A clean, simple layout and design provides a comfortable buying experience. Reliability is also essential, since it speaks for the credibility of the store and the safety of the transaction. Flexibility is key, since customers often change their minds and either drop, add, or exchange items before making their final purchase. The cart can also store items for immediate checkout or hold them for a period of time. It is also necessary to have shopping cart software that tabulates amounts, such as shipping and taxes.

A Yahoo! shopping cart can match the look and feel of the Web site. When customers locate an item to purchase, they can check a box or click on the product to add it to their Yahoo! shopping cart. At any time, customers can go to the cart to view items being stored, add more, or remove those they have decided not to purchase.

Yahoo! Merchant Solutions automatically creates a shopping cart and customer checkout pages based on simple forms that the merchant completes. Then, it is possible to easily customize the checkout pages to make them visually consistent with the Web site's design and layout. Depending on the level of monthly service with Yahoo!, the store owners also have the option of adding custom messages, fields, gift-wrapping choices, cross-sell recommendations, and multiple payment options.

Checkout pages include the shopping cart, shipping and billing information, and order review and confirmation screens. The store owner can control how many of these pages are displayed and make sure that the checkout process is streamlined and meets customers' needs. Customers' shopping cart contents can be held for two weeks, giving them multiple opportunities to complete their purchase.

Payment Gateway

A payment gateway is a secure, private online pathway that payments take from the shopper to your store and its financial institution. The shopper authorizes a payment from his or her bank account, debit card, credit card, or PayPal account, or pays with some other method. The payment is then released by the appropriate financial institution before being submitted to the store.

Yahoo! primarily uses PayPal for the payment gateway, First Data, or a service already used by the merchant. Credit card verification and validation tools are offered, as is credit card processing. When customers put in their credit card numbers to pay for their items, the money is delivered to the vendor, but the credit card numbers are not transmitted. PayPal applies a different number to go through over the Internet to control fraud and risk. SSL offers the highest level of encryption supported by commercial web browsers and follows the standards established by credit card leaders such as Visa and MasterCard.

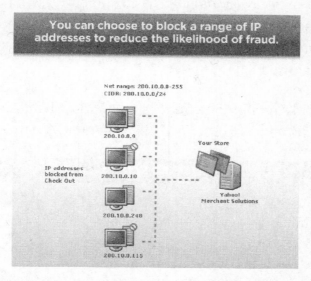

Reproduced with permission of Yahoo! Inc. ® 2009 by Yahoo! Inc. Yahoo! and the Yahoo! Logo are trademarks of Yahoo! Inc.

Order Processing System

Last but not least, stores must process customer orders and fill them to the customer's satisfaction. It is necessary to have an invoicing system in place that interfaces with an accounting program. The more professional the invoicing looks, the higher the likelihood of repeat orders. You will also need an inexpensive, effective approach to packing and shipping customer orders. There needs to be a designated area for packing and storing boxes awaiting pick-up by parcel services.

With the Yahoo! system, merchants are alerted of online purchases so the staff can prepare the order for shipment using the customer's selected method of shipping, such as U.S. Postal Service, United Parcel Service or Federal Express. The order system also compares the order against inventory and alerts the store owner to any necessary problems, such as last item in stock. Throughout the process, customers also receive alerts to let them know that their orders have been received and processed, and when they have been shipped.

These are only part of the offerings that Yahoo! has. Later, we will cover the whole lineup of services they offer for Merchant Solutions.

CASE STUDY: SHERRY COMES

Sherry Comes
President
CoffeeCakes.com
991 Pinefield Lane
Castle Rock, CO 80108-3622
1-800-830-2696
http://www.CoffeeCakes.com

"Since its inception, our Yahoo! store has enjoyed annual growth of about 30 percent."

One of the wonderful aspects of the Web is the variety of information, services, and products available. The e-commerce and community activities of the millions of online users world-wide show how diverse people are. The Yahoo! stores' products and services exemplify this diversity well.

Who would think, for example, that a Web store specializing in coffee cakes and related gift items would be such a sweet success? (Then again, who can pass up a warm, tasty piece of coffee cake?) President Sherry Comes, who founded **Coffee-Cakes.com** in 1995 out of Castle Rock, Colorado, says, "Since its inception, our Yahoo! store has enjoyed annual growth of about 30 percent."

CASE STUDY: SHERRY COMES

Originally, the company was formed as an Internet coffee shop, the first in Denver, but Comes quickly realized how much better she could do by selling her delicious coffee cakes and teamed up with Yahoo! to market exclusively online. Now, **CoffeeCakes.com**'s ever-expanding product line includes cheesecakes, whiskey cakes, rum cakes, travel mugs, and more.

When it comes to the Internet and other related electronic communication, Comes knows of what she speaks. An IT guru, she was involved with the online world well before most people even knew it was born. Customer service is the number-one reason why her company keeps growing. Repeat business is a large portion of sales. And each dollar brought in has more than the usual value attached to it. A portion of **CoffeeCakes.com**'s profits is donated toward research for Neurofibromatosis (NF) and to help support families affected by the disease. The Yahoo! store's support for this cause was prompted by the fact that Comes' son was diagnosed with the disease in 2005. Gillian Anderson of The X-Files is another spokesperson for the NF cause, and Comes and Anderson formed a charitable partnership that supports those affected.

The price of a Yahoo! store is one of the best deals available, according to Comes. What a merchant gets for such a small monthly fee is amazing, especially when considering how well e-commerce sites can do. That is, if the merchant does his or her share of the work. "People have to realize that it is not a 'Build it and They Shall Come' situation," Comes says. "Actually, it will be the opposite if a store owner does not invest the necessary time in the business. This is more than a full-time job."

CASE STUDY: SHERRY COMES

A job that has its rewards: Comes received the 2008 "Outstanding Women in Business" award from *The Denver Business Journal* and the National Association of Women Business Owners.

E-commerce Success

Here are several things to keep in mind when considering your future business.

- The Internet may be a new technology, but business principle basics are not any different from brick-and-mortar stores. You need to provide high-quality goods and/or services that customers or clients want and at prices they can afford, but that also allow you to make a profit.

- You need to know how to market to online shoppers. Always keep in mind the keywords your customers or clients will use to search for your products or services.

- Your best customers are those who have shopped with you before, online or off. You want to keep them coming back for more. Cultivate them by maintaining regular contact and offering them special information and occasional specials as your preferred customers.

- Make your Web site easy to use, so shoppers can begin

buying as soon as they arrive at your site. Point them in the right direction with a link that says "Shop Here" or "Begin Shopping Now," so there is no question how to begin.

- Web site designers are good at creating an attractive, useful Web site, but make sure it works for both you and the customer. Every site and audience is different. Is yours easy to use and navigate? Does it meet your particular users' needs? Test it before it goes live, and make adjustments if needed. Also, listen to the customers' feedback as to what works well for them, and what they would like to see change.

- Consider making your site handicapped accessible. It will be more costly, but the time is coming when all Web sites will have to come up to code. If you code your site correctly, and place in correct attributes for individuals with screen-reading programs, you will get new customers. Doing the proper disability coding makes the site more text-oriented and raises a site's search engine rankings.

- Ensure that you offer a secure Web site that protects your customers' privacy. Use an opt-in e-mail system, so that you are only e-mailing potential and existing customers who have agreed to accept information from you via e-mail. If you plan to share your e-mail list with others, disclose this to your subscribers.

- To protect yourself and your customers, keep an eye out for fraudulent orders (more on this in a later chapter).

Planning Your E-commerce Site

Before creating your Yahoo! store, spend some time planning it out to be sure that it will meet the following objectives:

1. Generate new customer prospects

2. Bring in new sales

3. Improve customer service

4. Build relationships with existing customers or clients

- Keep these objectives in mind as you map out the site's navigation and prepare content for your site.

- Always have an "About Us" section that provides information about yourself and your business, so new visitors get a sense of what your company is and what it is about. People want to buy from an actual "person," not from a "company." Give them a phone number to call for further information or with questions. Include "real" customer testimonials, news, and other related information to create an identity to which your customers can relate.

- Make sure that purchasing information is clear (e.g., pricing, shipping, terms and conditions, delivery, and relevant guarantees). Provide product information that is easily accessible and has the relevant information required (e.g., dimensions and compatibility) so that customers can make informed decisions.

- Include keyword-rich text so that search engines can easily find your Yahoo! store and index it appropriately for your market niche.

- Engage prospects and customers by providing an easy-to-use, interactive online experience.

Next Steps

E-commerce is really just another avenue for buying and selling products and services. It may use fancy lingo or newer technology, but like other business basics, e-commerce can be mastered. Armed with this knowledge, you can create your own Yahoo! store, which we will explain step-by-step in the next chapter. We hope this introduction to Yahoo! has provided enough substance to whet your appetite. There is much to cover, so let us begin.

CASE STUDY: MARTY FAHEY

Marty Fahey, CEO
OrderMotion, Inc.
129 South St
Boston, MA 02111
1-877-775-3900
http://www.ordermotion.com

No one said running a business is easy. The financial and personal rewards are great, but it takes considerable work. One of the most time consuming activities is all the backend work. OrderMotion, out of Boston, specializes in organizations with five to ten employees that process over 25 orders per day. The company lends software support that enables merchants to take orders, manage inventory, and process payments via one easy-to-use interface.

Patrick Puck, founder and CTO, comes from a background of large-scale mail order solutions and processes, as well as call center, data entry, warehouse, and IT implementations supporting retail commerce. He developed OrderMotion services, such as application development, database construction and management, and back-end programming. Marty Fahey, CEO, has a strong technology background and from the start, saw e-commerce as a way to "rock the traditional retail world." When he was given the opportunity to head up OrderMotion in 2007, he "was excited to inherit a great product and brand in the e-commerce industry."

"Yahoo! also provides the means to scale your e-commerce business to whatever heights you wish to reach."

CASE STUDY: MARTY FAHEY

Yahoo! has partnered with OrderMotion for many years, "because Yahoo! Merchant Solutions continues to be the best place to start an e-commerce company," states Fahey. "It has great tools to build a Web store that are flexible enough to create a distinctive brand. Equally important to many Web merchants, you can be up and running very quickly. Yahoo! also provides the means to scale your e-commerce business to whatever heights you wish to reach. And the power of the Yahoo! Merchant Solutions' community in search results makes merchants far more visible to the search engines inside Yahoo! than they would be on their own."

The OrderMotion service simply plugs into a merchant's Yahoo! store when they reach a volume where their e-business that requires automation to grow. "Our system brings you the same tools the big e-tailers use to speed their processing, lower their customer support costs, and increase their profits. Our clients can manage inventory, automate customer service, launch revenue generating marketing campaigns, and handle customer accounts and histories," adds Fahey. The services provided are priced to support all levels of revenue and are delivered through a Web browser, so clients do not have to invest in hardware, software, or additional IT.

OrderMotion has about 300 clients, ranging from $500k businesses to some that have grown to $50 to $60 million, with about half of them either still using or having used Yahoo! Merchant Solutions. "If you are just starting out," states Fahey, "you do not need us yet. We like to joke that customers come to us when success is driving them crazy. It's when they start needing a warehouse, when service calls are becoming too much, and when they haven't seen the kids for a while! Normally, that point is around $500k to $700k in annual revenue."

CASE STUDY: MARTY FAHEY

Fahey recommends that Yahoo! store owners make marketing their number-one focus. It is easy to get caught up in all the other operational issues surrounding a Web store and forget to constantly "obsess about attracting more customers and selling more product. We always suggest choosing good partners to support your operation, so that you can stay focused on what's really important — revenue."

CHAPTER 3

Are You Ready to Yahoo!?

Yahoo! offers many opportunities, and thousands of people have found it a valuable part-time or full-time investment or business. That does not mean this type of business, or any business of your own, is right for you. Many people have no desire to go it on their own, away from the often more stable nine-to-five full-time jobs. Also, even in these virtual days, numerous individuals have no desire to spend their time online, let alone start an Internet business. There are still many traditional retail stores, businesses, and service operations being started in the "real" world.

Starting a business online has some similarities with opening up an offline enterprise, but there are a number of important differences. You need to give a good deal of thought to your personal goals and interests before deciding whether to go e-commerce, regardless of whether it is with Yahoo! or another online store. If you are uncertain, you can always start out with a small amount of products and then build up, and as you will see, Yahoo! gives you that opportunity. One of the positives of going with Yahoo! is that it only takes a small investment to find out whether you want to change your life in a big way.

Do not forget that if you start a business, be it an offline "brick-and-mortar" shop, a Yahoo! Store, or any other kind of online

Web site, you are looking to generate income — otherwise, it is a hobby. Bottom line: starting a store takes considerable work. One of the ways that online businesses are pitched is through commercials that promise the world. First, the more time you put into your business, the better it will do. You cannot expect to put in an hour a day and get a windfall. Second, it takes time to build an online business, for the same reason it does to grow a brick-and-mortar one. People have to find out that you exist and can offer the products they want. It will take about two to three months just for you to get a listing on Google, and that is if you spend considerable time writing editorial for the search engines.

Building up a Business

Nothing in life comes without its advantages and disadvantages, and running an online business is no different. Creating an online Web store, even with the support of Yahoo!, will demand ongoing set-up and maintenance time. For instance, as you will see, you have several months of work before you even are ready to design your Web site. You need to choose a product or service with a positive future, position your business, develop a marketing plan, name your business, decide on a Web site URL, find a vendor for your products, get a license to sell, determine your shipping options, and check about taxes and a zoning permit. Then, depending on how many products you order, it will take considerable time to get all the items uploaded, your Web site completed, and the marketing plan started with your kickoff event.

There are also a few other things to consider. You cannot always have the same products for sale, so think about how you will be altering your product line in the future, and the way you will provide incentives with marked-down items and sales. Also, realize that the line "build it and they shall come" does not apply here. With millions of Web sites online, buyers do not know to come to your Yahoo! store, unless you tell them that you are up and running. Online marketing is different from the traditional approach; there is no tried-and-true way to promote a Web site. Even the online Gurus say that you have to use several different types of marketing approaches to bring buyers to your store. Marketing your site takes at least a couple of hours of work a day and, perhaps, some money to invest for product advertising.

Also, keep in mind, that you will be your own boss, as with any self-employment. There is no supervisor to keep track of what time you arrive or a time clock that records when you come and go. You have to push yourself. When that alarm goes off in the morning, it is easy to turn over and go back to sleep, because you only have yourself to worry about. When you are in your home office and feel the warm breeze coming through the window, or hear your kids playing outside or the baseball game on the TV next door, it is very easy to take a break "for just a few minutes."

You have no one but yourself to maintain the discipline of putting in the necessary hours for work. You need to motivate yourself to work a certain amount of hours every day, set and review your own goals, and establish and follow your set schedule. Some people have no problem shutting out the distractions and getting the work done, and others frequently find excuses to be away from the office. Some individuals cannot wait to be working on their own. Others have no desire to be self-employed, because they like the security and not having to think about work 24/7, 365 days a year.

There are also certain skills and abilities that go along with running your own business, and time management is one of the most important of these, since you will be wearing a number of different hats. Time management goes along with multi-tasking, as well as the need for organization. Think about the people who work with you at your regular job — the accountant, secretary, marketing manager, shipping and receiving personnel, product ordering clerk, and maintenance and security people; in your own business, all these roles are yours, and more. There is also another crucial part of your work —education. People who succeed in their own business are continually keeping up to date about their industry and looking at trends on what they need to do to insure continual business growth. In addition, the online world is always changing, which means you will be regularly updating your business strategy and marketing plan.

Finally, another major difference between off- and online stores is that even when you will be spending most of your day interacting with customers and vendors, this will be over the phone or through e-mails or instant messaging. I have been working with people for five or six years, and we call each other friends, but we have never met. We may never meet. The communication and relationships that take place in the virtual world are quite different from those offline. Some individuals like this aspect of working online and do not miss the daily communication with other employees. Others feel too alone and get a part-time job to interact with people, or go back to full-time work.

This overview about working on your own is not meant to be discouraging, but realistic. It is important to know the advantages and disadvantages when you make such an important decision. There are many people who love the challenges of being on their own and do not like working for others.

A Number of Advantages for Online Business

Let us look at the other side of the equation now. There are a number of benefits of starting an online business, and many merchants, like those in this book, say that they would definitely make the same decision if they had to do it all over again. The number one plus is personal satisfaction and pride. There is something to be said about setting and accomplishing goals on your own. It is quite gratifying to see those orders come in. With all the reports and data you receive from Yahoo!, you have the ability to make changes and quickly see the impact that those changes will have on your customers' buying habits.

Here are some of the other advantages:

- As noted above, you are your own boss, manager, and supervisor. You do not answer to anyone except yourself. You decide the hours you want to put in and the goals you want to reach. You can work out of an office in your house or rent an office in another building.

- Your store is always open, so you decide your best hours. Go to work in your PJs. Get up real early in the morning, when the house is quiet and there is no one to bother you, or work while the kids are at school and again after they go to sleep.

- You have to put in considerable work, but the rewards are all yours. You are not sharing the income or only allowed so much out of each sale made — with the exception of Uncle Sam, that is.

- No more commuting back and forth — and paying for all that gasoline — or waiting in long hours of traffic. When working until 8 p.m., you are at your own place, rather than knowing you will not be home for another one to two hours. You cannot take off every day, but when something special comes up with the family, you know that you will be there.

- This is not something that you have to achieve over night. Start working part-time on Yahoo! while still in your regular day job. When your income grows enough to meet your expenses, then leave your full-time position. It may be difficult doing both jobs at the same time, but you will see the light at the end of the tunnel. If you are uncertain this is the type of work for you, you have the time to find out.

- It would be difficult to find another business you can start with such little investment. As Sherry Comes of CoffeeCakes.com said, she could not believe it was possible starting a business on such a small amount of money. "It was one of the best kept secrets!" You have a low monthly payment to Yahoo!, and the products can be paid for after they are sold. Your overhead is the cost of equipment you probably already have, as well as your advertising. If you start part-time, you will have little outlay.

- You may not be working with anyone in your home office, but over at Yahoo!, there is a whole team of people who are working on making life better for you. They offer a host of features and services, and they are continually working on new ways to promote your business. Yahoo! did not get its positive reputation by sitting still. When other companies were failing, they kept running smoothly.

- The computer may be off when you are asleep, but that does not mean your business is closed. Automation is a wonderful innovation. Someone across the world can go shopping in your store, even when you are not around. Just let the auto responders, e-mail systems, and automated credit card businesses run your store. This is one of the most attractive aspects of owning an Internet business. It takes over for you when you are offline.

- The Yahoo! store you open is not only selling to people in your town, state, or even country; it is selling to shoppers worldwide. Your potential market can be as wide as you want. You decide on your buying audience and how it will be reached and captured.

- All studies show that e-commerce will be growing significantly for another decade. It may not be as much of an increase as over the past ten years, but definitely enough to do quite well — about 20 to 40 percent growth, depending on the industry.

- The Internet is bursting with information and experts who are giving free or low-cost information on how they became successful. If you spend time with others in the field on forums, blogs, e-zines, and e-books, you can get valuable help with your business. Some of the people who are involved with the Internet are unbelievable in their ability to see what is around the bend and to prepare for it way in advance.

- People all over the world have different interests. Not everyone is going to want your product, but there will be enough who do. Just think of how many millions of people are presently buying online and the numbers coming aboard every year.

- Especially if you connect with a marketing-oriented company such as Yahoo!, you can more effectively reach a much larger pool of potential buyers specifically looking for your type of product.

In short, the decision to create a shopping cart for your products online or sell a service will depend on numerous intimate facts about your personal goals, work habits, interests, type of industry, and resources. The case studies in this book will also give you a better idea of how other people made this decision and some of the successes and challenges they have had along the way.

Here is a good business readiness assessment tool from the U.S. Small Business Administration (SBA) to help determine whether you are ready to start a business. To access the online version, and to have the SBA automatically tally your score, visit **http://web.sba.gov/sbtn/sbat/index.cfm?Tool=4**. This interactive tool will review your answers and make suggestions as to how to turn your answers from "No" to "Yes."

Answer "Yes" or "No" to the following questions:

General
- Do you think you are ready to start a business?

- Have you ever worked in a business similar to what you

are planning to start?

- Would people who know you say you are well suited to be self-employed?

- Do you have support for your business from family and friends?

- Have you ever taken a course or seminar designed to teach you how to start and manage a small business?

- Have you discussed your business idea, business plan, or proposed business with a business coach or counselor, such as a faculty advisor, SCORE counselor, Small Business Development Center counselor, or other economic development advisor?

- Do you have a family member or relative who owns a business?

Personal Characteristics

- Do you consider yourself to be a leader and a self-starter?

- Would other people consider you to be a leader?

- Are you willing to invest a significant portion of your savings or net worth to get your business started if you need to purchase inventory and equipment?

- Do you have enough confidence in yourself and your abilities to sustain yourself in business, if or when things get tough?

- Do you like to make your own decisions?

- Are you prepared, if needed, to temporarily lower your standard of living until your business is firmly established?

- Do others turn to you for help in making decisions?

- Are you willing to commit long hours to making your business work?

- Would others consider you a team player?

Skills, Experience, and Training

- Do you have a business plan for the business you are planning to start?

- Do you know and understand the components of a business plan?

- Do you know what form of legal ownership (sole proprietor, partnership, or corporation) is best for your business?

- Do you know why some consider business planning to be the most important factor in determining your business success?

- Do you know whether your business will require a special license or permit and how to obtain it?

- Do you know where to find demographic data and information about your customers?

- Do you know how to compute the financial break-even point for your business?

- Do you know how to compute the start-up costs for your business?

- Do you know about the various loan programs that are available from banks in your area and the SBA if you need money to get your business started?

- Do you understand how a business loan can impact your credit?

- Do you know how to prepare and/or interpret a balance sheet, income statement, and cash flow statement?

- Do you know why small business loans are considered more risky than loans made to large businesses?

- Are you sure your planned business fills a specific market need?

- Do you know your target market?

- Do you understand the tax requirements associated with your business?

- Do you know how to prepare a marketing strategy for your business?

- Do you know how to learn about your business competitors?

- Do you understand marketing trends in your business industry?

- Do you feel comfortable using a computer or other technology to improve business operations?

- Do you have a payroll process planned for your business?

- Do you have a customer service strategy in mind or in place?

- Do you know how to obtain an Employer Identification Number (EIN) for your business?

- Do you know whether your business should have some form of intellectual property protection?

- Do you know where to obtain information about regulations and compliance requirements that impact your business?

How did you do? Are there areas that you could improve upon? If you have concerns after taking this test, meet with a counselor from your local small business development center to see how you can fill in the gaps with training, education, or other business resources before taking the leap to self-employment.

Now, let us assume you have decided that you want to start your own business. You have come up with a viable idea that you are excited about and that seems to fill a need for online shoppers. Congratulations. You are now ready to learn more about Yahoo! and you.

CASE STUDY: KEN KIKKAWA

Ken Kikkawa
President & CEO
eHobbies
877-eHobbies (346-2243)
http://www.ehobbies.com/

Events can be both pro and con, depending on the person and circumstances. When the dotcom bubble burst, eHobbies started exploring options to liquidate. Ken Kikkawa says "I was already working for the company and fortunate enough to be able to acquire the assets of what remained. I right-sized, overhauled the business model, and got up on the Yahoo! platform." At that time, the company had an enterprise solution and maintained a Yahoo! store that it designed in parallel with the main Web site. "Yahoo provides a robust and flexible platform for design and back-end user interface," stresses Kikkawa.

Since then, he has had outside designers and contractors continually customize the site, product search, and shopping cart. "One of the great things about Yahoo! stores is that there is an entire business environment that exists for development. Either Kikkawa or one of his colleagues has used all of Yahoo!'s services. Over the years, he has updated "multiple times," as new technologies and features have become available. "This year, we upgraded our site search, unveiled a new site design, and implemented product reviews. We're continually evolving and improving."

"One of the great things about Yahoo! stores is that there is an entire business environment that exists for development."

CASE STUDY: KEN KIKKAWA

The company is continually growing, primarily, says Kikkawa, "because we listen to our customers. We implement features they are looking for, bring in products they want, and provide them with the service they deserve. Yahoo! has provided a very solid platform on which to both start and grow a business." If a company is looking for a robust, inexpensive, and flexible platform that will allow for growth, then Yahoo! is the answer.

Kikkawa tells new Yahoo! store owners to establish a plan and vision, be vigilant about taking care of customers, make friends with others via networking, and always get second opinions before implementing big decisions.

Get Going

Maybe you are weary of your nine-to-five job, or perhaps you would like to escape corporate America to start your own business. Or maybe you just want to earn a little money on the side with your favorite hobby or pastime. If you have considered starting your own business and controlling your financial future, you are not alone. According to the Small Business Administration, in 2007, 14 million Americans were self-employed.

Thanks to Yahoo!, your dreams of owning a business can now become a reality. Whether you want to dabble in your own business part-time or are ready to jump in full-time, Yahoo! offers the services and tools you will need to get started.

The first step in business ownership is perhaps the most obvious — deciding what type of business you want to own. For the purposes of this book, we will assume that you want to open an online store to sell products and/or services. Perhaps you are embarking on business ownership for the first time, or maybe you already have a mom-and-pop brick-and-mortar shop and want to expand your business. Either way, our focus will be on launching, managing, and growing an online Yahoo! business.

Consider what you want to sell: products, services, or maybe a mix of the two. If you do not already have an idea, start by thinking about what you know. Are you an expert golfer or a knitting hobbyist? Perhaps you possess a love of books. From a service perspective, maybe you have considerable marketing knowledge, writing talent, or shoe repair skills. Make a list of your areas of interest, and see whether one of those topics ignites a passion in you. To put it simply, if you are going into business for yourself, be it part-time or full-time, your new venture should be something you will enjoy.

Now that you have a list of ideas, let us examine the criteria needed to evaluate a business idea. Here are some questions to ask yourself:

- **Will you succeed as a business?** That is, can your potential business consistently earn a profit? If not, the Internal Revenue Service may define it as a hobby, and you cannot deduct your business expenses.

- **Will you meet your financial needs and goals?** If you want this online business to be your only income, your idea must cover your expenses. If it is part-time income, what kind of income potential do you need your business to produce for it to be worth your while?

- **Will you meet your personal needs and goals?** How will your business fit into your life style? What type of work schedule can you guarantee? If you plan to launch your business full-time from the start, can you devote enough time? Do you plan to be available 24/7, or just Monday through Friday, nine to five?

- **Will you match your interests, skills, and abilities?** When choosing a business, you need to know your strengths and weaknesses. What interests you? What skills and abilities can you bring to a new business? Do you have the skills needed to launch your own business?

- **Will you be able to put your business in motion now?** Based on the criteria above, do you have the ability to start a business now, or do you need to take some other steps first to ensure your success? For example, maybe you need to keep your full-time job a little longer to save money for those first few not-so-profitable months (or years), or perhaps you need to take some classes to learn about finance and business planning, merchandising and inventory management.

Passing the Online Test

If your business idea passed these five steps, it is time to do some research to see whether the idea is viable in the online marketplace. What keywords best suit your business idea? Are those keywords popular? To help determine what keywords people search on the most, try an online keyword search tool, like the Google Adwords keyword tool, available at **https://adwords.google.com/select/KeywordToolExternal**. Try entering a search phrase, like "antique trains," for example. Google will return information on that keyword phrase, as well as similar phrases, including advertiser competition, the previous month's popularity for those keyword phrases, and average search volume. Google will also give you a list of suggested keywords for consideration.

From your own experience, and that of your friends, neighbors, and family members, do you see a niche that needs to be filled or a product that online stores seem to be lacking? You might start by asking others this question, "What do you wish you could buy online?" Based on their responses, go to Yahoo!'s Shopping Mall at **http://shopping.yahoo.com/**, and search for the suggested items. How many stores sell those items? Is there significant competition, or is there room for another store that could beat competitors on price or service? In other words, if you select this particular idea for your business, how will your store be different?

Next, consider your business idea from the customer's perspective. By selling your product or service online, what benefits can you offer your customer? Can you save your customer time or money? Can you supply a rare item that is difficult to find or allow your customers to purchase something online that they need or want, but will not travel to a store to get (think holiday shopping)?

Does your product or service translate well to the Internet? Keep in mind that with the Internet, you are limited to the seeing and hearing senses, so your products or services must appeal to your online customers on those levels. To get a better sense of this, poll your friends on whether they would purchase the items on the Internet that you are considering selling.

Once you have settled on a few of ideas, check out potential sources for your products or services. Where can you buy the desired products wholesale for a low enough price to make a profit after your overhead and expenses are covered? Consider manufacturers, wholesalers, and drop-shippers as potential sources. Contact a few of them to see what type of arrangements you can work out to keep your inventory at appropriate levels, and discuss how you might finance your purchases. Are there enough suppliers to choose from that your idea can become profitable?

Niche Products

When e-commerce first started, you could sell anything, and there would be people coming to your site. Now, however, there is so much competition among Web stores, and such a need for specific items that fit the unique interests of the consumers, that increasing numbers of stores are going toward the niche, or even the niche of the niche, product line. Forget baby furniture, for example, and look specifically for a site selling nothing but strollers. A site that only offers light bulbs is lighting up sales. There is even a site that only sells adhesive tapes.

Niche stores are growing fast. If you want to get an idea of all the different types of items you can sell online, check out Worldwide Brands, at **www.worldwidebrands.com**, and see their case study at the end of the book for some insights. Merchants who are just going online, or seriously considering it, should stay away from huge markets, such as **"BigJim'sHugeMegaitems.com,"** and forget trying to reach all the people all the time. It is difficult to offer the range of products at the same or a lower price to match the retail giants.

Instead, choose one section of one aisle of the big box stores, and sell as many products in that specific category as you can. In short, find an underserved niche in a market area, and be the one place to go for products in that niche. Pet clothing may have been big a few years ago, but now, you may need to specialize in a niche such as pet costumes, cat sweaters, or high-end pet fashion. Check out the following case study about **GreekGear.com**, and see how he continues to find niche upon niche.

Finding the right niche has several advantages:

- It is quite possible that you confront less competition than going against large retailers in crowded markets. Of course, you do not want to get so specialized that there are few or no buyers. For example, it is unlikely that many people want to order a case of sauerkraut pizzas or the latest earrings for cats. Nor do you want to sell something that does not interest you. Remember, you have to promote this business, learn everything about it, and become the expert for others.

- Shoppers are more apt to be enthused and engaged with a niche. If you serve an extremely targeted area, it may be easier to zoom in on these buyers by posting to forums, buying ads in newsletters, and catching them through blogs. Communities often form around these specialized topics. One of the primary differences with the Internet is that groups do not have to meet in person. Make it your goal for every relevant group, mailing list, forum, or community gathering to mention your store as the place to go for that unique niche of product and information.

• The search engines are going to love your copy. Your keywords and key phrases will be more specific, which may mean they are less competitive in terms of natural search ranking and of more interest to the search engines.

Next Steps

After reviewing the material thus far in this chapter, you will likely either feel energized and eager to proceed or unsure whether you are ready for such a big career change. If you are energize, let's now cover some business basics. We will explain what you will need to know and do before actually starting your business.

If you are still unsure, do not panic. Set this book aside for a day, a week, or a month. When the mood strikes you — or you are really frustrated with your day job — pick it up again. You just might find the motivation you need to move forward. No matter what your choice, we wish you success, and will be here when you are ready.

CASE STUDY: JOSEPH TANTILLO

Joseph Tantillo,
President and CEO, GreekGear
6 Commerce Drive
Freeburg, IL 62243
618-539-9998
www.greekgear.com

"Owning a Yahoo! store is not just a hobby to do in one's spare time. If you really want to be successful, you have to make it happen."

"Niche" is an important word for e-commerce. When merchants are fortunate enough to find a niche that sells, they are not only able to grow the original Web site, but can spin off with "niches of the niche," so to speak.

In 1999, Joseph Tantillo, president and CEO of Greek Gear, found his niche, starting an online business that specialized in Fraternity and Sorority Greek clothing. He opened a Yahoo! store because "it was the best option," he recalls. Since then, Tantillo has grown his "niche" idea into a $3 million business with 20 employees, 4 million customers, and over 15 different sites. Tantillo initially sent out all production, but soon learned that purchasing his own equipment was the key to keeping up with demand, controlling costs, and better serving his customers.

"We grow about 30 percent per year and are always trying new ways to expand." For example, this year, he saw competition mounting and his growth slowing down, so he invested in changes to his Web design and organization.

"The Web site is where it all starts, and a place on which we have to continually stay focused." With that said, growth is back to normal.

CASE STUDY: JOSEPH TANTILLO

Tantillo, as with other successful e-merchants, emphasizes that a site does not just grow by itself. "Owning a Yahoo! store is not just a hobby to do in one's spare time. If you really want to be successful, you have to make it happen."

Tantillo adds, "You need to have a positive attitude and keep trying new things. Even at down times, it is necessary to do research on ways to build the business." He sees the Internet as a way that anyone, regardless of background, can succeed. "It's a great equalizer. And, it's a great way to quickly see the results of your efforts. By making a change for the better on my site, I can see almost immediate results."

Some of the Fraternity and Sorority Greek related sites are:

- Greekgear.com
- SigmaChiGear.com
- TKEGear.com
- ThetaChiStore.com
- Greekpages.com
- DivineNineGreek.com
- SigmaAlphaEpsilonGear.com

Tantillo has also expanded his niche concept to other markets in which people are passionate. From their nationality, with Italian-based Web site, Guidogear.com, to their spiritual faith, with their popular Web site, Christiangear.com, and even to dog lovers, with GearforGoldens.com. Tantillo's goal is to open a new niche Web site every year. Considering he has nearly 20 Web sites to date, he is way ahead of schedule.

CHAPTER 4

Getting Started: Business Basics, Part 1

E very successful business starts with a well-organized plan. In this chapter, we will discuss the basics of starting your own business, including everything from naming your business and establishing it legally to licensing and zoning. We will go over business entities, how to develop a business plan, and how to market your business. We will show you how to use Yahoo! to build your online business from the ground up.

If you are feeling overwhelmed at this point, do not worry. Your feelings are completely normal. You are embarking on an exciting new adventure, and it will take considerable hard work to get your business set up. To help ensure your success, we will make the process easier for you, providing you with step-by-step instructions, checklists, and resources along the way.

Establishing Your Business

From the exercises in the previous chapter, let us assume that you have selected a viable business idea and you feel that you have the skills, training, and motivation to launch a business successfully. For the sake of discussion, let us assume that you have selected a product line of ten office gadgets that you want to sell in your Yahoo! store. You have arranged to work with a drop-shipper in South Carolina, who will package and ship purchased items to your customers. The preliminary details are in place. It is time to name your business, select your business entity, and explore local licensing and zoning laws.

Choosing the Perfect Name for Your Business

We will begin with naming your business. Short and sweet is always a good starting point, but consider something catchy too, something that shoppers will remember and can spell easily. The name of your business should clearly let people know what products or services you sell. Do not try to be too witty with a play on words that is spelled differently. If you have already named your business, you want your Web site to have the same name. That way, if people think of you, they know exactly where to go online. Your name needs to be memorable and pronounced and spelled easily, and make sure that you are not infringing on any trademark. To be sure your name is not a copyright, visit **copyright.gov** and search before you buy.

Avoid using a hyphen and numbers, and be careful about using "my," "the," or a similar word in front of the name, such as "**mycookieshop.com**" or "**thedogbone.com**," and plurals, such as "**bluejeansstore.com**." If you need to do this, because your name is already taken, then be sure to always use the full name in all your promotions. Do not say, for example, "Be sure to come to dogbone for all your puppy's food," when the name of your store is "**thedogbone.com**." Similarly, if you cannot get your business name with ".com," and must use ".net" or ".org," be sure to always use the full name: "Be sure to come to **thedogbone.net** for all your puppy's food." You should try your best, however, to get a .com name.

There are several reputable online sites, such as **GoDaddy.com**, where you can register names. Many names are available, and others are either for sale or auctioned off. If you already have a name in mind, and the registration company says it is taken, check it out. Perhaps it is for sale. Check its history, since you do not want a site that once was shut down for spamming or other infringement. There is much to be said about looking for a domain name first and then naming your business. This way, you can write down six key words that describe your business and play around on the registration site to see what is available. If you want to provide travel information and services, for example, you have words such as "travel," "trip," "excursion," "destination," and "vacation."

To choose a name that suits your business, spend some time brainstorming to see what names you can invent. If you need help, search online for existing businesses with similar offerings, use your dictionary or thesaurus, or ask your friends or family to help you come up with ideas. Another idea is to develop a list of adjectives that describe your business (e.g., fun, professional, dreamy, or expert) and consider using those in your business name. Always think about your niche and the keyword that will drive people to your site. Does one word strike you as being ideal? Next, apply the criteria above to see whether the name you have selected fits each one. If so, you may have a winner.

Here is Dana's example that shows you the "dos" and "don'ts."

She named her business *Virtually Yourz* in 2004. It is registered in the State of Washington, and she uses it for all of her non-publication, client-related work. When writing for publication, she uses her legal name, Dana Blozis. Her business name conveys that she provides services virtually. It is timeless, easy to pronounce, pleasing to say and hear (at least to me), and does not violate any existing trademarks. She likes the name and has used it for years, but it is not perfect. It does not convey that her business offers writing, editing, and marketing services. It is also not easy to spell. She chose the unusual spelling because the domain name **VirtuallyYours.com** was already taken. However, she has branded her company with this name (with a Web site, business cards, letterhead, marketing materials, and more) and must learn to live with its shortcomings. Her point is that you should choose your business name and the name of your Yahoo! store carefully. Ideally, you will be using it for a long time.

Yahoo! itself is a good example of how to select the perfect business name. The popular Internet portal did not start out with that name. In fact, it started out with a name (Jerry and David's Guide to the World Wide Web) that sounded more like a book title. As the company's popularity grew, though, a new, catchier name was needed. According to Yahoo! folklore, Yahoo! is an acronym for the phrase "Yet Another Hierarchical Officious Oracle," but Yahoo!'s history page says that founders Jerry Yang and David Filo liked the definition of yahoo described as "rude, unsophisticated, uncouth" as noted in *Gulliver's Travels*. Regardless of the reason for the name's selection, Yahoo! is easy to say and spell and is recognized around the world.

Just remember to be patient. The idea for your name might appear before your eyes in a matter of minutes, or it could take days or weeks. No matter how long it takes to come up with the perfect name, though, it will be worth it — particularly since you plan to be successful and will need to use it for many years to come.

Selecting the Appropriate Business Entity

Next, decide what type of business entity is most appropriate for your business. Per the Internal Revenue Service (IRS), you have the following options:

- **Sole Proprietorship** — A sole proprietorship is an unincorporated business owned by one individual. Many small businesses are sole proprietorships that name their businesses something different from their own names. For example, Dana might start a business called My Fabulous Antique Trains. Her business would be officially registered as Dana Blozis d/b/a (doing business as) My Fabulous Antique Trains.

- **Partnership** — A partnership exists when two or more individuals enter into a business agreement where each contributes a share of money, property, and/or labor or skill to the business and will share a proportionate level of the business' profits or losses.

- **Corporation** — In a corporation, shareholders contribute money and/or property in exchange for a proportionate share of the company's capital stock. A corporation can be privately held or traded on a public stock market following an initial public offering (IPO). ABC Corporation, Inc. is an example of a corporate name.

- **S Corporation** — Eligible domestic corporations can elect to become an S corporation, which is taxed more favorably than a regular corporation.

- **Limited Liability Company** — Known as an LLC, the limited liability company is a relatively new business entity. Like a corporation, the owners have a reduced risk of liability for the company's losses and actions, but other features are similar to partnerships (e.g., management flexibility and pass-through taxation). Most LLCs use that moniker in their name: My Antique Trains, LLC.

For advice about your specific situation, contact a business consultant, accountant, or attorney. Additional information is available at **www.irs.gov**.

Business Licensing

This is by far the most confusing aspect of starting a business. You need to be sure that you have the proper licensing for your business. The major types you will need to familiarize yourself with are:

- **Local Business License:** This is mainly for a retail brick-and-mortar business, specifically. In some communities, this license will run about $25, but in some larger communities, it runs in the hundreds.

- **State Business License:** This is also known as the state sales tax license. This license is required for Internet sales, because you will need to collect sales tax. With customers that live in the same state as you, you will need to collect the tax and then pay it to the proper state agency at the end of the quarter. You will need this license before you can buy goods from a wholesale supplier without having to pay sales tax on the goods.

- **Sales Tax Number:** You will need this number, and it will be given to you when you get your sales tax license. Without this number, wholesale companies will likely not do business with you; if they should happen to, they will charge you a sales tax on your goods purchased. This is a charge you cannot recover from your customers if you do not have a sales tax number. When you buy your goods, you want to at least get your money back with the sale. When companies receive this sales tax license and their tax number, they usually have it printed on their letterheads and invoices. This makes it easy to find, and it will already be accessible for the wholesalers or/and any other companies that you deal with.

- **Employer Identification Number (EIN) Number:** You will use this number if you decide to sell advertising space on your Web site. You will also use it if you:

  o Hire employees

  o Incorporate

  o Form a partnership

You will use this number in place of your social security number. You will provide this number to the companies that are paying you to run advertisements on your site.

You can obtain this number right away by calling the Business and Specialty Tax Line of the IRS. You will receive a hard copy by snail mail, but you will receive the number when you call.

States are actively trying to get Congress to pass legislation for all sales made on the Internet to be taxed. So far, only businesses with a gross less than $4 million a year are exempt, but look for this to change. You should err on the side of caution and collect all the required taxes and pay them to the proper Federal and State agencies. Note what each jurisdiction requires, how often renewals are required, and how much each license or permit costs. You will want to add this information to your business budget, discussed later in this chapter.

Zoning laws will also apply. Many small businesses, particularly service businesses, can be housed at home without violating local zoning laws, but check with your local jurisdiction to be certain of the requirements. You might be appropriately zoned for a home-based business, but you may not be allowed to put up signage or invite clients or customers to your home. Retail and warehouse locations will require commercial or mixed-use zoning. Keep this in mind when getting licensed and selecting the location for your business.

Developing a Business Plan

Most prospective business owners cringe at the term "business plan." This is primarily because developing a business plan seems dry and boring compared to naming a business, buying inventory, and setting up your Yahoo! store. It is a time-consuming document to prepare, but a business plan is a necessary component for success. A well-written, well-organized plan will not only assist you in guiding your business through its birth and beyond, but it is necessary if you hope to obtain investor support or bank or government financing for your business idea.

Although formats can vary, a good business plan contains four sections: 1) a description of the business; 2) your marketing plan; 3) current and projected finances; and 4) a management plan. The components of a business plan include the following:

The Business

- Description of your business

- Marketing

- Competition

- Operating procedures

- Staffing

- Business insurance

Although formats can vary, a good business plan contains four sections: 1) a description of the business; 2) your marketing plan; 3) current and projected finances; and 4) a management plan. The components of a business plan include the following:

- Business Overview

- Public Relations and Marketing

- Competition

- Operations

- Employment

- Insurance

Financial Data

- Financial institution loans

- Equipment and supplies

- Balance sheet

- Margin of safety

- Profit and loss statement

- Three-year review

- Monthly breakdown for year one

- Quarterly breakdown for year two and three

- Projection assumptions

- In- and outflow of cash

Supporting Documents

- Past three years tax returns, with personal financial statements

- Franchise, lease, and purchase contracts

- Licenses and permits

- Principles' vitae

- Letters of intent from relevant parties

In addition to these items, your business plan should include a cover sheet, a mission statement or statement of purpose, and a table of contents, so interested parties can quickly find the items that concern them.

Creating a Budget

When creating a budget for your new business, it is important to understand that it is a projection of income and expenses over time. As you start your business, it is helpful to budget for at least a year out, perhaps two or three. Begin by outlining each of your expenses (overhead, staffing, inventory, and insurance, for example) for the time period selected. Next, project your income for the same period. Remember that in the first few months — perhaps even the first few years — your business may not turn a profit. This is frustrating for many business owners, but particularly those who quit a full-time job to open their store. They may be used to that full-time income and have to temporarily adjust their standard of living or reduce their personal expenses to make up the difference.

The initial goal, of course, is to at least cover your expenses. To begin, record all of your anticipated expenses for the coming year. Your list should include items like rent or lease payments, utilities, inventory, insurance, staffing costs, shipping costs, marketing, advertising, office equipment and supplies, hardware and software, Web site expenses, quarterly taxes, and Social Security payments. Next, list what income you hope to make each month for the same period. When you first start your business, estimate conservatively. The first few months will most likely be slow, and it could take you a year or longer to turn a profit. This is typical, so try not to get frustrated.

Now compare the two lists (income versus expenses) to see whether your projected income will match your expenses. If not, consider other sources of income to keep your business, and family, afloat in the meantime. Do you have savings you can tap or spousal income? Can you take a part-time job to supplement your income until your business is successfully turning a profit every month?

When Dana first started her business, she had some outside income to help with expenses as she grew her business. She supplemented that income with a flexible, part-time job. After a year and a half of juggling her schedule and income and expenses, she comfortably went full-time, and has not looked back since.

Business Capital

Unfortunately, nothing is free or easy in this world, and this includes your Internet store.

Starting and running any business is not easy. It involves hard work and takes careful planning, organization, and capital (money).

As we mentioned briefly above, one of the things you will definitely need is capital (which is cash). The main reason to mention capital is finding sources, whether out of your pocket or from an investor (business or person). The goal is for your business to grow, and when it does, your capital source must also. No matter what the size of your online store, in order for your business to grow, you need to have a business plan for a this growth.

Business plans outline the goals that you have made for your online store. And as your business grows, so does your business plan. It will be changing periodically with updates and new goals (milestones) for you business, especially when your business becomes larger and/or if you decide to take your part-time business to a full-time business.

If you decide to go to a full-time business, you will need additional capital. A "formal business plan" will be needed to approach a funding source, whether it be an investor or a bank loan.

A formal business plan includes:

- Complete financials (including a *proforma*, or a three-year financial projection of revenue and expenses).

- Cash flow and income statements

- Balance sheet

It would be a good idea to have these financial documents, regardless of whether you decide to apply for funding. They keep you informed on your cash flow in and out.

Wholesalers and Distributing Companies

Drop-shipping can save you a substantial amount of money (capital) in your business. This type of shipping for your products essentially eliminates the need for warehouse storage. When you are creating your online store, advertising and marketing your products, and maintaining your site, every amount of savings matters.

There are good resources to help you find companies that will help you in locating various products. The following Web sites will lead you to information on products to buy at wholesale prices, advice on how to buy products at wholesale prices, and a list of manufacturers that are willing to drop-ship your products to your customers' shipping addresses.

- Wholesale World: **www.wholesale-world.us**

    o This site is a good resource on finding products to buy.

    o At this site, you will also find an extensive list of many popular product categories, and their extensive list of wholesale-supply companies that carry these different products.

- How to Buy Goods Wholesale: **www.wholesale-worl.us/ retailers.php**

- Drop-shipping Manufacturers: **www.wholesale-world. us/drop-ship.php**

Also see the case study for Worldwide Brands.

CASE STUDY: PATRICIA GIADONE

Patricia Giadone, President
Children's Organizers
785 E2 Oak Grove Road #105
Concord, CA 94518
1-800-510-9860
www.childrensorganizers.com

Yahoo! storeowners come from a wide variety of different backgrounds, both virtual and offline. Patricia Giadone, president of Children's Organizers, left a money management company in 2007 to find a balanced life of work and raising a family. She is pleased to report that she successfully manages her time and is able to wear all the separate homemaker and Yahoo! e-commerce hats. "I started working at night after the kids went to bed. Now that they are both in school, I have the opportunity to work during the day as well," she explains. The additional hours make it easier to handle the time-consuming business activities, such as carefully selecting new products that will be a good fit for her store and making sure that each of the product descriptions and images on her site make for an easy-to-understand, enjoyable experience for her customers.

> ### "As soon as you can optimize your site for your key products, your placement in the search engines begins to rise."

Marketing her site also keeps her busy. Search engine optimization is an ongoing process that involves understanding which keywords shoppers are likely to use in any given search. "As soon as you can optimize your site for your key products, your placement in the search engines will begin to rise," Giadone states.

CASE STUDY: PATRICIA GIADONE

In addition, she currently markets her store among several different channels — e-mail, newsletters, pay-per-click advertising, and print advertising, in addition to posting new, relevant product data to the Children's Organizers blog.

Children's Organizers carries preschool / daycare furniture as well as kids' bedroom furniture and decor. The mission "is to provide early childhood educators and parents with high-quality, discounted furnishings and supplies for kids," as well as the tools to create a structured, fun environment for the children to learn, explore, and be creative.

Giadone cautions potential Yahoo! store owners that "they have to love the merchandise they are selling. It's a great deal of effort getting the store the way you would like it." Giadone has done much of the technical work herself, plus turned to Yahoo! Web site designers to beef up such features on her site as the shopping cart, with the goal of keeping the visitors longer. "Starting an online store is a big learning curve for people new to e-commerce," Giadone admits, "but it is well worth the effort from both a business and personal standpoint."

CHAPTER 5

Getting Started:
Business Basics, Part 2

Developing a Marketing Plan

Depending on the size of your business, a marketing plan can be an extensive, detailed, lengthy document, or it can be as simple as a list of marketing goals for a particular year, scheduled by month or date, and a marketing budget. We will go through both to get an idea of what type will better suit your business.

Regardless of the format of your marketing plan, you will want to keep in mind your strategic position, which specifically spells out why your business is one-of-a-kind. Why do customers/clients want to come to your site versus others? When defining your company's strategic position, look at such factors as trends in your industry, how you compare to the competition, technology changes, and your niche strengths.

You must ask yourself questions such as the following when determining your strategic position:

- What do future trends look like for your product/service?

- How can you position your organization in the future?

- What opportunities can be seized and threats met?

- How can this be put into practice in a systematic way?

- What is your audience now and how can that be expanded?

- What ways will you sustain and expand your business?

Part 1: Your Purpose, Mission, and Vision

This portion of the marketing plan should briefly explain the purpose of your marketing plan. For example, are you creating it to outline your new business strategy for the short- or long-term? Maybe you already have a business, but you are adding a product line or shifting your marketing strategy. Regardless, state the purpose of your marketing plan clearly and succinctly.

Mission Statement

Next, consider the mission of your company. This should be a brief, carefully crafted message that tells customers and other stakeholders what your company does and what it believes. It also sets a standard of expectation for a company's employees. As you create your statement consider including some or all of the following concepts:

- The moral/ethical position of the company

- The desired public image

- The key strategic influence for the business

- A description of the target market

- A description of the products/services

- The geographic domain

- Expectations of growth and profitability

For example, here is a very specific mission statement for a fictitious airline company:

ABC Airline, Inc. will be viewed as the most state-of-the-art venture in the air transportation business. It will offer business customers cost-effective and high-quality transportation service on the East Coast and will guarantee a return on investment and growth rate consistent with current management guidelines.

Vision Statement

A vision statement is a snapshot of what the company foresees for its future. It includes a brief, concise, and promotional statement of what it plans on attaining. The vision statement is frequently stated in terms related to competition in the marketplace. Vision refers to broad objectives, which are all-encompassing and progressive. It describes the goals it needs to reach, as well as future expectations, without providing the specifics on how these will be attained.

The goal of ABC Airline, Inc. is to be the premier provider of business air transportation on the East Coast. Our focus is to provide cost-effective and high-quality transportation with a superior product and outstand-

ing service. Our commitment is to continually develop these products and services to enable our clients to meet their ever-changing goals.

Part 2: Situational Analysis

This section of your marketing plan will contain a detailed analysis of items that will affect your business. It will include an analysis of the following business components:

Product and service mix

What products and services will you offer to your customers?

Target market, including demographic data

To whom will you offer your products and services? What niche(s) will you target? What demographic best describes your ideal customer?

Distributor network

How will you deliver products and services to your customers? Yahoo! offers a variety of standard and overnight shipping options.

Competition

Who are your competitors, and how will you differentiate your business from theirs? To locate online competition, do an online search for businesses using the same keywords you have selected. Look at their Web sites and review their products, services, prices, strengths, weaknesses, and market segments. How are you different?

Finances

Consider factors such as your potential sales, marketing expenses, and profitability.

Environment

How will the environment affect your business, its products, and its services?

Summary

Analyze your business with a SWOT (strengths, weaknesses, opportunities, and threats) analysis to give you an overview of your current market position.

Part 3: Marketing Strategy, Marketing Objectives, and Financial Objectives

In this section of your marketing plan, you will outline marketing and financial information. From a marketing strategy perspective, you will project market growth and stability, outline costs, and prepare an exit strategy for a particular market, should it prove to be unprofitable. Next, you will review your marketing objectives, covering such topics as market share, customer base, sales, promotional and channel objectives, market research, and research and development strategies. From a financial perspective, you will explore customer and channel sales, margins, profitability and financial ratios, and metrics.

This section might also include a discussion of the niche market(s) you have selected. Different businesses, of course, define niche markets in different ways. Some options to consider when defining your niche include industry or business type, demographics, unique expertise, style, and geography.

Part 4: Tactical Information

This part of your marketing plan will cover tactical marketing programs, target markets, product and promotion plans, and distribution and pricing strategies. Here, you will discuss the details of your marketing strategy or, put another way, how you are going to reach your marketing goals. These are the details of your plan.

Part 5: Budgeting, Implementation, and Performance

Here, you will outline your company's marketing budget for the next financial period (calendar or fiscal year). Based on your marketing strategies in Part 3 and tactical marketing programs outlined in Part 4, how much will your marketing program cost?

Further, you will want to do a performance analysis to determine the return on your investment for your marketing dollars. Your analysis should be broken down into marketing performance, a break-even analysis, and common marketing ratio analyses (e.g., advertising to sales).

How will you measure each component of your marketing plan? And finally, when do you expect to implement each marketing tactic?

Part 6: Additional Factors

In the last section of your marketing plan, you should list any pertinent items not included elsewhere in the plan. For example, are there internal factors that could affect your company's success (e.g., change in staffing and loss of investors)? Are there external factors that could affect your business, such as problems with a supplier and increased shipping costs?

Finally, list any research limitations or assumptions that affect the information included in your marketing plan. Are all the assumptions based on beginning the plan January 1, 2009, for example? Do they assume your competition will not change between now and then, or that your overhead costs will remain the same for a certain period of time? Include any factors or assumptions that are critical enough to point out for consideration.

Small Business Resources

At this point, you probably realize that starting a business is hard work. Whether it is a brick-and-mortar or online business, it takes a great deal of time and commitment to succeed. What spurs people, despite all this work, is the fact that the more you put into this business, the better your business becomes. Many of the individuals who are highlighted in this book's case studies have established a high-income business through the use of Yahoo! and their dedication. You can do the same, since the online world offers millions more opportunities. Developing a detailed business plan is an essential element in your success. Do not hurry through this phase, because it sets the foundation of all your future work.

If you would like additional support as you work through this process, rest assured, there are countless resources available to you as you embark on your new business venture, many of which are low cost, or even free. Consider the following resources:

- **America's Small Business Development Center Network**
  www.asbdc-us.org
  America's Small Business Development Center Network represents member Small Business Development Centers in supporting small businesses throughout the United States. Its Web site offers informative articles, news, and links to useful resources and services for small business owners.

- **The National Small Business Association**
  www.nsba.biz
  The National Small Business Association was founded in 1937 to serve as an advocate for small businesses in the United States. The organization now represents more than 150,000 small businesses.

- **SCORE**
  www.score.org
  SCORE (Service Corps of Retired Executives) is a non-profit organization made up of more than 11,200 volunteers with more than 600 business skills. As a partner of the U.S. Small Business Administration, SCORE assists small business owners by offering resources such as advice and training.

- **The U.S. Small Business Administration**
  www.sba.gov
  The U.S. Small Business Administration is an independent agency of the U.S. government that aids and protects the interests of small business in the United States.

You may have other resources in or near your community as well. Check area community colleges, local chapters of SCORE, small business development centers, chambers of commerce, small business owner organizations, networking groups, and economic development organizations. If they do not have the resources you need, they can likely point you in the right direction.

Next Steps

Now that you have established and named your business, obtained the appropriate registration and licensing, created a budget, and developed business and marketing plans, you are ready to learn more about Yahoo! and how you can apply all of these specifically to building your Merchant Solutions store.

CASE STUDY: JOHN AND AMBER WESTERMAN

John and Amber Westerman, Owners
Pop Deluxe!
310 State Street
Madison, WI 53703
608-256-1966
http://www.popdeluxe.net

John and Amber Westerman, owners of Pop Deluxe!, a store with products running the gambit from children's toys to household items and pet supplies, swear by the saying "Never put your eggs in one basket." Although their store near the University of Wisconsin in Madison is growing every year, they "truly believe that the future of retail involves the important element of online shopping. Even on the sunniest day in bustling downtown Madison, we can only reach a certain amount of traffic. By adding the online Web store, Pop Deluxe! is now available to millions of eager shoppers 24 hours a day!"

The Westermans started working on their online store in 2006. Amber had always been intrigued by graphic design and computer programming, so it started as a hobby. "I loved the idea of translating the look, personality, and philosophy of Pop Deluxe! into an online form. It's a challenge because we're constantly reinventing ourselves." John started studying web optimization "and the fun really started!" they agree.

The couple decided to go with Yahoo! "since it's a household name, harmonious with online shopping."

The couple decided to go with Yahoo! "since it's a household name, harmonious with online shopping. The big boys out there don't just choose their partners 'willy-nilly.'

CASE STUDY: JOHN AND AMBER WESTERMAN

There's a lot of research, thought, and money that goes into it. Seeing some larger retailers working with Yahoo! made us very comfortable," they say.

The Westermans like that Yahoo!'s site building and back-end management systems are easy to use. One common fear for small retailers is the lack of control when building and maintaining a Web shop, especially when the inventory is changing so rapidly. How do you have a site that reflects your own personal style and stock? "Starting out, it's scary to think of having an outside company managing your site. How will they photograph everything? How will they know how to best describe and sell your products? No one knows your shop and style like you do," adds Amber.

Yahoo! provides an affordable way to do it yourself. "The key is their amazing staff. You can find most answers on their online help, but they also have a live 800-number with a very knowledgeable staff to answer any questions." When the Westermans first designed their site, they used the Yahoo! program Site Builder. "Creatively, it was a great tool. But if you need to make lots of changes or add a lot of products regularly, it is laborious. The Yahoo! staff suggested we switch to Store Editor. It's extremely easy to manage your items and keep them looking organized. The drawback is that it's based in RTML, and the templates are rather limiting in their natural form."

To help out, they hired RTML programmers to make necessary changes. The best feature is store owners can add a la carte features to their site or get creative help with their design. "There are some really talented people out there that are experts in writing RTML code. One of the greatest things you can learn in running a small business is how to ask for help!" stresses Amber.

CASE STUDY: JOHN AND AMBER WESTERMAN

The Westermans also use the Yahoo! analytic tools quite a bit, as well as e-mail lists, newsletters, and a blog.

They have not signed up for Yahoo Marketing, "although it looks like a great program with lots of incentives for merchants."

The results show the hard work the couple puts into their site. They report that "The response has been fantastic and overwhelming. Because we invested a lot of blood, sweat, and tears, it's incredible to see it doing well and growing at a rapid rate. We offer very personalized service, so our biggest compliments come from our level of customer interaction. We truly see it as an extension of our brick-and-mortar shop, so we pride ourselves on making the site fun and friendly."

The Westermans warn new or prospective store owners that they should be "ready to work! Once you get going, it's easy to feel like working on your site 24 hours a day. It's exciting, challenging, and addictive. You'll start waking up in the middle of the night, looking for the magical glow of the 'red asterisk,' indicating that you've got orders."

When people already have an existing brick and mortar, they know all the challenges and many little details a store presents daily. "Your Web shop is no different — just a change in format. It takes constant care and passion to keep it fresh and up to date. Customers notice if you don't change your store windows or displays. Same goes online. Keep mixing it up, even if you think no one is watching." Adds the couple, "the most important thing to remember is how large your audience is out there. Stay true to your unique style, and your customers will find you. Providing great service will keep them coming back."

CHAPTER 6

Choosing Your Yahoo! Plan Level

Thousands of merchants around the world have chosen to open Yahoo! stores in categories including beauty, books, clothing, computers, electronics, flowers and gifts, general merchandise, health, home and garden, jewelry, music, sports, and toys.

There is a reason so many merchants have chosen Yahoo! for their online stores — it is easy to set up, use, and navigate. You can set up your store in less than 24 hours, even if you are not technically savvy. Perhaps more importantly, Yahoo! is affordable, offering different merchant plans ranging from $39.95/month to $299.95/month.

In addition to its ease of use and affordability, Yahoo! also commands significant traffic. Nielson Online continually ranks Yahoo! in the top ten parent companies in terms of Internet audience metrics. It was only topped by Internet giants Google and Microsoft.

Let us start with an overview of the Yahoo! services you will want to consider when opening your first (or next) online store: Web hosting, domains, merchant solutions, and online marketing.

A la Carte Online Services

One of the advantages of choosing Yahoo! for your online services is that you can purchase exactly what you need. Do you just want a domain name while you research starting your own business? No problem. Or maybe you are ready to open your Yahoo! store now and want the full range of Yahoo! services at a package price? Yahoo! offers that option, too. The services can be purchased individually or as a package. For example:

- Domain names can be purchased for $9.95/year each.*

- Web hosting with domain name purchase is available in a package starting at $11.95/month.*

- Full merchant service packages can be purchased starting at only $39.95/month.*

- Yahoo! offers a variety of online marketing services at different price points. You select what services you want (e.g., pay-per-click) and how much you want to pay for them.

The best part is that you are in control of your Yahoo! experience. You choose what you want to spend each month based on the services you want and what you can afford.

Comparison Chart

Key Features

	Custom Mailbox Sign up	Business Mail Sign up	Web Hosting Sign up
Price			
Annual fee	$34.95/yr		
Monthly fee		$9.95/mo	~~$11.95~~ **$7.77/mo.** For your first 3 months.[1] ($11.95/month after)
One-time setup fee		**$25 setup fee**	~~$25~~ WAIVED [1]
Email			
Number of email addresses	1	10	1,000
Storage space per account	Unlimited NEW!	Unlimited NEW!	Unlimited NEW!
Email attachment size	20MB	20MB	20MB
Access email using a POP client like Microsoft Outlook® **	Yes	Yes	Yes
Get even more email addresses	No	Yes	Yes

*Pricing is subject to change. For up-to-date pricing, visit Yahoo! Small Business at http://smallbusiness.yahoo.com/ Reproduced with permission of Yahoo! Inc. ® 2009 by Yahoo! Inc. Yahoo! and the Yahoo! Logo are trademarks of Yahoo! Inc

Web Hosting and Domain Names

Every new business needs a Web site and the basic components to create and maintain one, including Web hosting services, a domain name, and business e-mail accounts. Yahoo! provides all these services for small businesses with three different plans: starter, standard, and professional.

Ranging in price from $11.95/month to $39.95/month with a $25 set-up fee, these plans each include the following:

- Disk space: This is the number of Web pages that your package will support. It ranges from 5GB to 20GB of data transfer monthly. Another way of determining this is that the packages allow 10,000 to 1.2 million visitors per month.

- Business e-mail addresses: 200 to 1,000 unique e-mail addresses

- Domain name search and purchase (e.g., **www.yourbusinessname.com**) and easy-to-use design tools to create your Web site

- Support for third-party design tools like FrontPage®, Dreamweaver®, and Microsoft Publisher

The level of each service offered depends on which package or plan you purchase. For example, with the starter package, you can have between 5 and 25,000 Web pages. That is less disk space than a business owner who buys the professional package, but probably more than adequate for most merchants' needs.

What is particularly nice about Yahoo!'s Web hosting packages is that you get a variety of services and product features for one low price, with no hidden charges or fees. As a new business owner, this will help you establish a monthly budget and determine your break-even point. You want to make enough money to at least cover your costs each month, and anything above that will be considered profit.

Yahoo! also offers e-mail access from anywhere, 24-hour customer support, and reliable, secure hosting. What is even better is there is no annual contract for Yahoo!'s Web hosting services. You can upgrade or cancel your plan at any time, so there is no risk.

You can transfer an existing domain name, if you already have one. However, you will be responsible for renewing the registration. You can also obtain a new name through Yahoo! for no additional charge. When you secure your domain name as part of Yahoo!'s Web hosting services, you receive 24-hour customer service, domain name registration, locking, forwarding, and complete domain name system control.

This means that Yahoo! will help you search for your desired domain name, it will lock that name in so it cannot be stolen by someone else at renewal time, and it will forward your domain name to an existing site, if you desire.

Keep in mind that the Web hosting and domain name package discussed above is the most basic of Yahoo! services. It is an ideal solution if you are just beginning to plan your Yahoo! business. It is affordable and can be upgraded to another package later. If you are ready to create your Yahoo! store now, however, you will want to start with one of Yahoo!'s Merchant Solutions packages.

Web Hosting Design Gallery

Web Hosting includes two site building tools that allow you to build a professional-looking web site.

Reproduced with permission of Yahoo! Inc. ® 2009 by Yahoo! Inc. Yahoo! and the
Yahoo! Logo are trademarks of Yahoo! Inc

Merchant Solutions

To help business owners and entrepreneurs like you start their first online store, Yahoo! offers three comprehensive merchant solutions packages with dozens of easy-to-use, customizable features. The packages include the Web hosting and domain name services mentioned above, ranging in price from $39.95 to $299.50 per month, each with a $50 one-time set-up fee. Store owners are also charged a fee per transaction, from 1.5 percent to 0.75 percent, based on their anticipated monthly revenue and the plan they select.

Plan Differences

	Express Sign Up	Starter Sign Up	Standard Sign Up	Professional Sign Up
Monthly price	$19.95/mo.	$39.95/mo.	$99.95/mo.	$299.95/mo.
One-time setup fee	$50	$50	$50	$50
Transaction fee	2.0%	1.5%	1.0%	0.75%
Recommended plan if you expect sales of:	Up to $4K/mo.	$4K to $12K/mo.	$12K to $80K/mo.	More than $80K/mo.
Maximum number of products you can sell	10	50,000	50,000	50,000

*Note: Prices are subject to change
*Merchants should note that some features, such as cross-selling at checkout, are only available with the purchase of the Standard or Professional plans.
Reproduced with permission of Yahoo! Inc. ® 2009 by Yahoo! Inc. Yahoo! and the Yahoo! Logo are trademarks of Yahoo! Inc.

Let us discuss the various features of the three plans:

Starter: Recommended for monthly sales less than $12,000

Standard*: Recommended for monthly sales between $12,000 and $80,000

Professional*: Recommended for monthly sales more than $80,000

There is also another package called the "Express." With this account, the monthly price is $19.95. The set-up fee is the same $50 as all the others, but the biggest difference is the transaction fee, which is 2 percent. It is anywhere from ¼ percent to 1 percent more than the other plans, and recommended sales are no more than $4,000 per month. The maximum number of products is ten. This is a plan for an extremely small business. It is good for those who do not want to take a big risk or just want to try things out.

You can decide to go with a higher plan if you expect to generate more sales and have a lower fee per transaction. While the one-time setup fee is the same for all three plans, you pay much less per transaction in the Professional Plan. The transaction fee is 1.5 percent for the Starter Plan, 1 percent for the Standard, and 0.75 percent for the Professional. The recurring fee also differs. The Starter Plan costs the least, with a monthly recurring fee of $39.95 per month, the Yahoo! Merchant Solutions Standard Plan costs $129.95 per month, and the Professional Plan is $299.95 monthly. The Starter Plan may seem quite inexpensive, but it could be the Standard or Professional Plan that saves you money in the long run, if you plan on growing your business.

For example, the difference between the Starter and Professional Plan monthly fees is $266. The difference between the per-transaction rate of the Starter Plan and the Professional Plan is 0.75 percent, with the Starter Plan carrying twice the cost. If you have an average sale of $1,200 a day, you will pay $18 per-transaction fee per day if you are on a Starter Plan. On the Professional Plan, you will pay only half, saving $9 a day, or $270 a month.

If you already have a business, then look at your sales compared to the suggestions made by Yahoo! and see where you fit best. If you are a new business, then start at the beginner's level, watch your sales carefully, and be ready to make the move into the next level. There is nothing wrong with beginning at lower sales and upgrading with your business growth. The Starter Plan will ensure you have money when you need to conserve cash for essential expenses, advertising, and marketing. Keep in mind that there are some important features that you only get with the Standard or Professional plans.

- **Cross Selling:** Suggesting related products to shoppers, such as utensils with a grill, generates greater sales and profits. It also allows you to offer volume discounts on specific products.

- **Gift certificates:** By selling someone a gift certificate, you bring a new person to your Web site, which adds sales. You can consider giving a bonus to the person buying the gift certificate to thank him or her for the extra business.

- **Real-time integration with backend systems:** Yahoo! will automatically determine whether inventory is available when a product order is placed. It also calculates shipping and taxes automatically, which saves you having to refund sales when a product is not in stock and unnecessarily upsetting the customer. Also, you receive inventory alerts when quantities are low and can manage inventory by variables such as color and size. Real-time integration with backend systems is an essential feature, and is quite helpful if you can afford the extra cost.

- **Notification of new orders by fax:** This is helpful when you would like a fax sent to your dispatch department or warehouse, or if you cannot check your mail several times daily.

- **Export orders to UPS Worldship®:** This saves time, since you do not need to enter the name and address repeatedly, and eliminates entering a wrong zip code or address. Order processing is fast and error-free. You choose among shippers, such as UPS, FedEx, and USPS. You can set shipping rates by weight, price, and location and can offer free shipping. You can set tax rates by country, state, and zip code. You can ship orders to international locations and use UPS online tools.

- **Yahoo! Web Analytics for advanced, real-time reporting**: This is a unique system that shows how your customers are acting only minutes after they have made a decision on your site. Find out, for example, why someone exchanged one product for another or what keywords were chosen to look for a specific product.

CHAPTER 7

Yahoo! Tools and Services

Yahoo! offers simple, customizable site templates and building tools, so you can create your own design, or select one of 12 pre-designed themes, plus a host of developmental and operational tools to grow and run your business. If you do not find a design that fits your business, you may opt to use a third-party design tool, like Dreamweaver® or FrontPage, or you can hire a professional designer to help build your store for a fee. Designing Yahoo! stores has become such a popular business that some designers specialize in only building Yahoo! Web sites. Once you select your design layout, you can upload your logo and Web site content. Initially, you will create basic pages, including Home, About Us, E-mail, Site Map, Privacy Policy, and Shopping Cart. You can add new pages as the need arises.

Reproduced with permission of Yahoo! Inc. ® 2009 by Yahoo! Inc. Yahoo! and the
Yahoo! Logo are trademarks of Yahoo! Inc

Product Catalog

Whether you are selling your latest e-book or thousands of gift items, Yahoo!'s product catalog will help you to easily upload product data and pictures to your site with its Add Products Wizard. Using the catalog, you can load up to 50,000 products for sale with a simple online form. You will fill in the requested information, such as item name, description, price, and shipping options.

As an alternative to the Add Products Wizard, you can upload an existing product database or spreadsheet. This option is particularly useful if your supplier provides you with this data or if you already have a product database or spreadsheet.

Store Products Page Wizard

Yahoo! SiteBuilder lets you easily create a Store page with the Store Products Page Wizard, guiding you through the process step-by-step.

To create a Store page with the Store Products Page wizard:

1:

Enter text for the title of your page in the **Page Title** field. Enter text for the body of your page in the **Body Text** field. When you have completed this step of the wizard, click the "Next" button to continue.

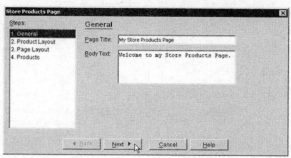

2:

Select a product layout you would like to use for the products on your page. When you have completed this step of the wizard, click the "Next" button to continue.

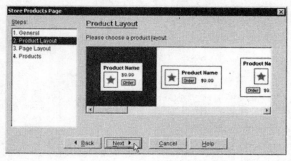

3:

Specify the layout of products on your page by using the "Columns" and "Rows" fields. Please note that the maximum allowed dimensions are 10 columns and 100 rows. Using the "Advanced Settings" section, you may further modify the page layout by changing the default spacing of products on your page. When you have completed this step of the wizard, click the "Next" button to continue.

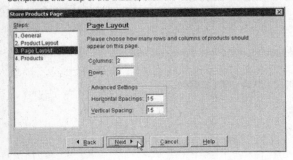

4:

Select one your product items from each of the pull-down menus. The order in which you select the products will be the order in which the products are placed on your page. When you have completed this step of the wizard, click the "Finish" button.

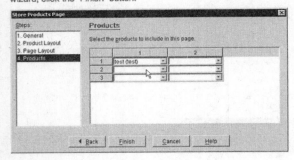

Shopping Cart and Checkout

Yahoo!'s shopping cart and checkout system allows you to easily create a custom checkout page for your customers, using one or multiple pages. You design the layout and determine the data fields you want to capture and Yahoo! does the rest for you — no coding required.

Customize your shopping cart and checkout process.

Quick Facts

- Easily customize your entire checkout process to maximize sales.
- Automatically calculate and display shipping and tax fees in the shopping cart.
- Offer gift wrapping and messaging options and sell downloadable products.

Help maximize your sales with our customizable checkout process.

With our checkout tools you can:

- Choose a single- or multi-page checkout process to help customers complete their sales process faster.
- Easily tailor your checkout page layout, fonts, colors, and buttons to match the rest of your site without any coding.
- Easily modify your checkout fields to collect information relevant to your business.
- Checkout pages are created automatically after you select your preferences - *no coding required*.

How do I set up my Shopping Cart?

View Demo ▶

Automatically calculate shipping, tax, fees, and discounts before checkout.

We calculate purchase totals in the shopping cart so customers can see exactly what they'll owe *before they check out*, eliminating a common frustration.

Encourage larger orders with cross-selling tools.

Set rules to display complementary products when a user adds an item to their shopping cart. For example, whenever a digital camera is purchased you can show batteries and camera cases as a cross sell.

Available with Standard and Professional plans only.

Save shopping cart contents so customers can return.

If customers leave your store without purchasing the items in their shopping cart, those contents are automatically saved for up to two weeks. Returning customers can then pick up where they left off and complete interrupted purchases.

Show customers where they are in the checkout process.

Display a progress bar at the top of your checkout pages to help prevent shoppers from leaving your site before completing a purchase.

Offer gift wrapping and messages.

Give shoppers the option to select gift wrapping services and leave personalized messages (if you offer them), and automatically add your gift wrapping fees to the purchase total.

Sell downloadable products.

Our flexible platform also allows you to sell non-tangible goods like downloadable products (such as software or music) or gift certificates.

For advanced customization:

Use CSS to apply a consistent design to your entire site. Update your entire site's appearance with changes to one central style sheet file. You can also use JavaScript to extract order data into third-party web analysis tools for greater insight.

Customer Service

Yahoo! supports its merchants every step of the way by offering 24-hour, toll-free phone and e-mail support, including free Web site setup consulting. In addition, Yahoo! provides detailed guides on how to get started, online help features, tutorials, and account manager assistance for qualifying accounts. Yahoo! is also known for its small business resources center, which provides help in a wide variety of areas.

Order Processing

With Yahoo!'s easy-to-use interface, merchants can process and track orders, view new orders online or via e-mail or fax, automatically e-mail customers with order status changes, and print invoices and UPS shipping labels. If you are already using an order management system, Yahoo!'s system can be integrated with yours so the two work hand in hand.

Shipping and Taxes

You set up the system one time with shipping and handling rates based on product weight, price, quantity, location, or other criteria that you choose. You can even offer free shipping or send products internationally. The options are entirely up to you, and you can make changes as needed. If you want to set up your own rates, Yahoo! will walk you through the steps of using a pre-determined rate table, like the one UPS uses. You can go to the UPS.com Web site and register. You will then be e-mailed an account number and be able to order shipping labels, boxes, and packing material. You will be billed at a later time, making start-up shipping an easier undertaking. When setting up your store's tax tables, you can input rates by country, state, and zip code. You input the data one time, and Yahoo! does the rest when an order is placed. Shipping and handling fees and taxes are automatically calculated at checkout.

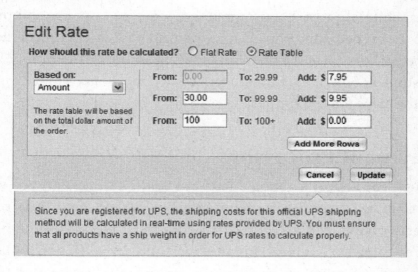

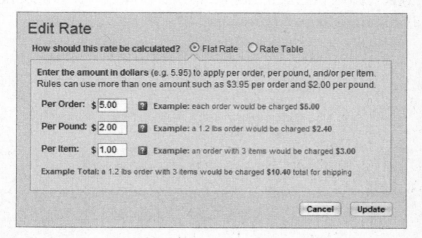

In the preceding charts, you can see that you have two simple setups for shipping rates. In the first table, you have an example of flat rate shipping to set a flat rate for different weights or the number of items being shipped. These also may be incentives for customers to move up to the next level if their price or item is close, or it will give them an incentive to buy the limit of items to their shipping cost. For example, suppose you have the shipping set up by item, and the customer's purchase is within the item amount, but not at the item limit for that amount of shipping. The customers will likely find an item or two more, since they will be at the same shipping rate.

Payment Processing

When you choose a Yahoo! Merchant Solutions package, you will be able to accept credit, debit, and PayPal and First Data payments online. Yahoo! charges no additional fees to use its payment gateway, but merchant fees may apply. In addition to these options, Yahoo! offers credit card verification, address validation, and offline credit card processing.

Reproduced with permission of Yahoo! Inc. ® 2009 by Yahoo! Inc. Yahoo! and the Yahoo! Logo are trademarks of Yahoo! Inc

Inventory Management

Yahoo! offers one-stop inventory management, an ideal tool to help online merchants manage their catalog of products. Based on data you supply and your sales to date, Yahoo! will track your product inventory and help you manage it by color, size, or other criteria you specify. You will receive inventory alerts when quantities of a particular product are low, so you can display inventory availability for customers (e.g., sold out, back order, or coming soon). You can integrate the Yahoo! inventory management system with an existing one.

Marketing

To support your business, Yahoo! offers a comprehensive marketing package to its merchants.

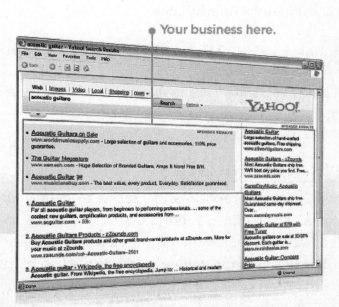

Reproduced with permission of Yahoo! Inc. ® 2009 by Yahoo! Inc. Yahoo! and the Yahoo! Logo are trademarks of Yahoo! Inc

Product Promotions

To highlight your store's products, Yahoo! offers product promotion features, including the following:

- Site search, so customers can easily locate products

- Discount pricing to build sales and reward customer loyalty

- Volume pricing to encourage larger purchases

- Incremental feature pricing, up-selling, and cross-selling* during checkout

- Optimized sales pages to increase product sales

- Gift certificates, coupons, and special promotions

- Trackable links for affiliates

- Product catalog XML read by shopping directories

*[*Cross-selling is only available to merchants who purchase the Standard or Professional package.]*

Reports and Statistics

Yahoo! also offers 40 reports and graphs to help you measure your success. The built-in reports assist merchants in tracking sales. Merchants can conveniently review revenue, items sold, number of orders, and top-selling items, as well as referring sites, the keywords used by site visitors, page-view information, and customer-click trails. With Yahoo!'s extensive report library, merchants can easily evaluate the success of their Web store, capitalize on products and site features that are working well, and improve on items that need adjusting.

Reports can be sorted by date, orders, revenue, and other criteria, so you can decide how to evaluate your data. You can also export the data into Microsoft® Excel® for further analysis and review. In addition, you can add tracking to your site to help you calculate the return on your investment. Options include:

- Measuring sales generated from your Yahoo! Sponsored Search listings

- Determining whether keyword advertising is profitable by tracking visitors

- Evaluating the success of any affiliate marketing programs you are using

Application Integration

Yahoo! is set up to work with external product and service providers for easy integration with other systems you are using. Features of Yahoo!'s application integration include:

- Compatible programs including QuickBooks, OrderMotion, UPS, First Data, and Stone Edge

- Export transaction information in QuickBooks, .csv, .xml, or plain text formats. (Available with Standard and Professional plans only.)

- Using Yahoo! with OrderMotion, merchants can create a multi-channel order management and fulfillment system for their online stores. Orders will be transferred immediately and securely from Yahoo! to OrderMotion for processing, avoiding duplicate entry.

- Yahoo! integrates UPS tools and services into its merchant solutions, so you can process UPS shipments and print labels directly from the Order Manager.

- If approved for a PayPal account, merchant accounts will be configured and integrated to process orders immediately. You can verify, authorize, or deny credit card transactions in real time, check an address to identify potential fraud, and automatically submit nightly batch transactions.

- Using Stone Edge, you can integrate Yahoo! to manage order processing and inventory management in real time.

Web Hosting, Domain Names, and Business E-mail Accounts

Each Merchant Solutions plan includes Web hosting features, free domain name registration, and business e-mail accounts, including the following:

- 20GB of disk space for your online store (Size and capacity may vary based on the merchant plan selected)

- 500GB of data transfer to support thousands of monthly store visitors (Size and capacity may vary based on the merchant plan selected)

- Free domain name

- Multi-user File Transfer Protocol (FTP)

- 200 to 1,000 e-mail addresses (Based on plan)

- Unlimited e-mail storage

- POP and SMTP support to set up your business e-mail for management by your e-mail program (e.g., Outlook)

- SpamGuard Plus protection to prevent unwanted e-mail (spam) from entering your inbox

- Norton AntiVirus™ screening to protect your e-mail inbox from receiving, automatically downloading, or forwarding computer viruses

Security

Yahoo! offers each merchant a security package, as well. The package includes Secure Socket Layer (SSL) technology with 128-bit encryption to protect transactions. It also includes credit card verification tools to help you identify fraudulent orders, in addition to the following:

- IP blocking to keep out suspect customers

- Web site password protection

- Varying levels of access privileges for site administration

- Extensive data center security to prevent your data from being jeopardized or stolen

- Compliance with Visa security procedures (CISP)

Web Site			
Number of web pages	1	1	Unlimited
Web site designs	8	8	390+
Web site customization	Partial	Partial	Full
Photos and logos	No	No	Yes
Drag-and-drop site-building tools	No	No	Yes
Domain name	Yes	Yes	Yes
Email Protection			
Norton AntiVirus	Yes	Yes	Yes
SpamGuard Plus	Yes	Yes	Yes
Filters	Yes	Yes	Yes
Blocked addresses	Yes	Yes	Yes

Reproduced with permission of Yahoo! Inc. ® 2009 by Yahoo! Inc. Yahoo! and the
Yahoo! Logo are trademarks of Yahoo! Inc

Reliability

According to Yahoo!, its Merchant Solutions supports one in eight online stores, processes more than $3 billion in transactions annually, and supports 2.7 billion shoppers every year. One of the reasons Yahoo! is so popular is that it guarantees that your online store will be up and running 99.9 percent of the time. For many new Internet users, high reliability is a given, but that was not always the case. Imagine creating a Yahoo! store that you cannot access whenever you want, or that goes down when Web traffic is high. Thanks to Yahoo!'s reliability guarantee, this is one aspect of managing your Yahoo! store that you will not have to worry about.

Your Yahoo! store will use and benefit from the same infrastructure as the rest of the Yahoo! network, with redundant links to the Internet backbone for faster access. Having your data backed up to redundant data centers in remote geographic locations means that your store's data can easily be restored in the event of a natural disaster or other emergency.

As part of your merchant plan, you will receive the benefit of other technological advances, like Akamai caching for faster product image uploading, a free BSD (UNIX) operating system, and Apache servers.

Online Marketing

In addition to the marketing and product promotion services offered in the merchant solutions plan, business owners can purchase additional online marketing tools from Yahoo!

One popular option is the purchase of a targeted Yahoo! ad. To utilize a Yahoo! ad, you create a text ad that will appear at the top of a search page when prospective customers search certain keywords on Yahoo!'s search engine. You decide how much you want to pay for the ad, and you only pay when the ad is clicked on, not every time it appears. The amount you pay for the ad is based on the maximum cost-per-click, or bid, that you specified when you set up the ad.

Reproduced with permission of Yahoo! Inc. ® 2009 by Yahoo! Inc. Yahoo! and the Yahoo! Logo are trademarks of Yahoo! Inc

Yahoo! averages billions of searches per month. By purchasing an ad, you can access a portion of this audience. With Yahoo!'s experienced support team, you can test different ads and get feedback on what keywords are the most searched. You can estimate results, track actual results, and target local or national audiences.

What is even better is that you can write your own ad, choose your keywords, and set a daily budget for how much you want to spend on pay-per-click advertising. If you are not satisfied with the results, you can stop displaying your ads or cancel your service at any time.

Setting up your ad campaign is simple. Follow these steps online or with the assistance of a Yahoo! representative, and your ads can be running in minutes:

1. Choose a geographic locale (international, national, regional, or local).

2. Select popular keywords that describe your business, products, or services (e.g., widgets, unfinished furniture, antique trains, perfume bottles, or hummingbird feeders).

3. Set a daily budget and a maximum price-per-click. You decide how much you are willing to pay (bid) each time someone clicks on your ad. You are only charged when someone clicks on the ad, not each time it is displayed.

4. Write your ad. It should include a title, a description of your business, and your store's URL (**www.yourstorename.com**).

5. Review and activate your ad.

Is Yahoo! the Solution for You?

As you can see, Yahoo! offers small business owners like you a wide range of affordable online services to open, manage, and market their stores. Other vendors exist, of course, but Yahoo! offers one of the most comprehensive, reliable merchant packages available. Overall, it is the most economical given all that it offers to its merchants.

CASE STUDY: CHRIS MALTA

Chris Malta, Founder/CEO
Worldwide Brands, Inc.
2250 Lucien Way, STE 250
Maitland, Florida 32751
1-877-637-6774
www.worldwidebrands.com

After spending several years as a Microsoft-certified systems engineer designing and building corporate and e-commerce networks, Chris Malta started looking for products to sell online. He quickly discovered that the search engines were full of scammers and "junk" directories, not genuine wholesalers.

"Through trial and error, I developed a process for locating and qualifying legitimate wholesalers who would work with online sellers like myself. To make a long story short, I realized many online sellers needed help finding reliable product sources, and **WorldwideBrands.com** was born."

...a full-time research staff dedicated to qualifying new suppliers based on the merchant's requests.

From day one, his company's product *sourcing* solution has been a natural fit for anyone using Yahoo's *selling* solution. Malta explains:

CASE STUDY: CHRIS MALTA

"We publish the Internet's largest directory of fully verified wholesalers and drop-shippers willing to work with online retailers. You get instant access to thousands of wholesalers, representing millions of quality products for stocking the Yahoo! store, with a built-in market research tool to help identify profitable product markets." The site also offers a full-time research staff dedicated to qualifying new suppliers based on the merchant's requests. The seller saves months of tedious, time-consuming research and trial-and-error learning.

Best of all, Worldwide Brands is not only for experienced vendors. The solutions are simple and user-friendly, and the Web site offers a significant amount of free education to help new online sellers. "Our sellers range from brand-new start-ups to retailers who sell millions each year," notes Malta.

He offers a tip to those who are ready for ordering products: "When you're selling online, the most important thing is to know that you're working with factory-authorized wholesalers. Whether you find them on your own or through a trusted resource like **WorldwideBrands.com**, working directly with 'real' wholesale suppliers and getting 'real' wholesale prices allows your business to be competitive in the online market and achieve the highest possible profits every time." The suppliers registered at Worldwide Brands have all been contacted and provided their contact information, order requirements, and Web site URL. "We've talked to each of these suppliers. They're expecting to hear from online sellers and are ready to work with them."

Put Up Your Storefront, Part 1

Congratulations. You are about to create and publish your first online Yahoo! store. You will find that even with little or no background in Web site development, you will be able to design your store. If you need help, Yahoo! customer service is available 24/7 to walk new users through the process. You will also be able to follow a written guide and tutorials. There is no better place to start than at the beginning, so let us get to it.

Opening a Yahoo! Account

To use Yahoo! Small Business Services, you will need to create a free online account first. If you do not already have one, we will walk you through it:

1. Go to **http://smallbusiness.yahoo.com/**.

2. At the top of the page under the Search box, click on "Sign Up."

3. A Yahoo! "Hi There" screen will pop up, asking for some unique identifying information. Fill in each section as re-

quested. The sections include (a) tell us about yourself; (b) select an ID and password; and (c) in case you forget your ID or password. Then follow the remaining instructions toward the bottom of the screen, which will ask you to (a) type code as shown; and (b) review and approve Yahoo!'s standard use agreement. When finished, select "Create My Account."

4. Yahoo! will return with a confirmation message and the details of your account (e.g., User ID). Print this page for your Yahoo! records. You may need to refer to it later. Your password will not print on this page, but a blank line is provided for you to write in your password. We recommend that you write it down. For privacy purposes, be sure you store this information in a secure place where it will not be easily found by anyone other than you.

5. Next, you will get an e-mail from Yahoo! at your alternate e-mail address. To activate your free account, click on the link in the e-mail.

Creating a Merchant Solutions Account

Now we want to set up your Merchant Solutions account. As discussed earlier, there are three types of plans: Starter, Standard, and Professional. Unless you expect to have more than $12,000 in sales revenue in your first month, or need some of the bonus features included with the Standard and Professional versions, we recommend you begin with the Starter package. You can upgrade at any time, if necessary. Let us create your account.

1. Go to **http://smallbusiness.yahoo.com**. Click on the "Mer-

CHAPTER 8: Put Up Your Storefront, Part I

chant Solutions" link.

2. Select "Plan Differences" in the bulleted menu on the left. Under the Starter plan, click on "Sign Up."

3. Put in your domain name. Yahoo! will return with a "Congratulations" message with a "Continue" button. Your domain will be maintained by a "registrar." This is a company that is responsible for "maintaining your domain registration records, managing your domain renewals, and other administrative details." The domain registrar for all of the new domains registered through Yahoo! is Melbourne IT. This partnership between Yahoo! and Melbourne IT allows you to have all the tools you need to maintain your domain yourself from your Domain Control Panel. There is also a domain database where you can find out who is your domain registrar. This database is WHOIS. You would use this service if you needed to find your registrar, you were going to move your domain, or if you were going to transfer a domain already created.

4. After you hit "Continue" in the previous step, Yahoo! may ask you to verify your e-mail password. Type in your password and select "Sign In." An "Order" screen will appear. You can complete the form as shown or call Yahoo!'s toll-free support line for assistance. This is where you will input your credit or debit card information to pay your $50 set-up fee and $39.95 monthly fee (starter plan fees). Fill in the appropriate information and click on "Continue." Yahoo! accepts Visa, MasterCard, Discover, and American Express.

5. Yahoo! will display your Domain Name Contact Information for your review and approval. The information as shown will be made public. If you wish for the information to remain private, you may select that option for a small monthly fee. On the right hand side of this screen, you have the option to edit your Yahoo! ID, Merchant Solutions Plan Details, and Your Domain Name. If no changes are needed, select "Continue."

6. Next, Yahoo! displays a "Billing Summary" showing what one-time and recurring fees will be charged to your credit or debit card. You will be asked to confirm or edit this information. Make note of this information for your business budget.

7. Review the "User Agreements" box, which will ask for your acceptance of Yahoo!'s policies regarding Merchant Solutions, Web hosting, Business E-mail, Yahoo! Mail general guidelines, and Yahoo! Store Merchant Guidelines. You also have the option to sign up for Yahoo!'s Small Business Newsletter. We recommend that you sign up for the newsletter to get tips and information on how to maximize your Yahoo! store.

8. Finally, complete the "How do you plan to use this service" box and click "Continue." As your order is being processed, a message showing that Yahoo! is processing your request will display at the bottom of the screen. It could take up to two minutes for Yahoo! to receive and approve your request. Do not hit the "Back" button, or you might get charged twice. When the order has been processed, you will receive an "Order Summary" that

you should print and save for your files. Then click "Get Started." You will have to sign in once again. Yahoo! will then ask you to create a "Security Key," in order to provide an additional layer of safety, and to select and answer a security question. Again, write this information down for future reference. Hit "Continue."

Stores built using our Store Design Wizard

Sites built by developers

Reproduced with permission of Yahoo! Inc. ® 2009 by Yahoo! Inc. Yahoo! and the Yahoo! Logo are trademarks of Yahoo! Inc.

Creating Your Web Store

Now comes the fun part — where you get to create the gateway to online sales success. A screen will pop up titled "Getting your store open for business." You have five activities to choose from here: (a) design your site; (b) add products; (c) payment methods; (d) set up tax rates; and (e) set up shipping. You can follow the steps in any order. Yahoo! will track your progress and let you know when you are ready to publish your site to the Web.

1. Let us start with designing your site to create a store layout for your Yahoo! store. Estimated time to complete: 30 minutes. Required materials: your company logo and company colors. If you choose not to design your site using Yahoo!'s tools, you can use other compatible Web tools or hire a designer who specializes in creating Yahoo! stores. Prices for outsourcing the design of a Yahoo! store vary from hundreds to thousands of dollars. If you want this option, consider getting recommendations from existing Yahoo! merchants. Each developer offers different services and prices, as well as experience, quality, and expertise. If you want help, call several developers Yahoo! suggests (also see case studies in this book). You want to go with someone with whom you feel comfortable and who you know will work closely with you. Some communicate mostly by e-mail and others by phone and e-mail, which is also a personal preference. Also, some work more with larger, more established stores and others, with new and developing ones. Look at their designs and call some of the store owners who have used their services.

2. Next, Yahoo! allows you to design a site using a generic template that you complete yourself or a pre-designed template with pre-determined layouts, color palettes, and pre-selected images. For now, we will start with a pre-designed template.

3. You can choose from 12 Yahoo! templates. Click on each thumbnail to get a better view of the design and review the template notes on the right side of your screen. These notes will guide you in the right direction for your store.

4. Yahoo! next gives you the opportunity to create the header for your site. This title bar will appear at the top of each page of your Web site. You can use plain text or upload a corporate logo. This is a good spot for your company name and perhaps your company's tagline. Here are some sample stores to check out: A Quilter's Notion (**http://store. aquiltersnotion.com**), A1 Health (**http://a1-health.stores. yahoo.net/index.html**), Hummels at a Discount (**http:// www.hummelsatadiscount.com**), and Taylor University Bookstore (**http://store.taylorbookstore.com**).

5. You now have the option to add text to the following pages: Home, About Us, Privacy, and Copyright. You will want to prepare this text in advance to speed up your store's design time. Here are some suggestions of what types of text or information you will want on each page.

Home page: Since this is the first page your visitors will see, it should be well organized, be visually appealing, and contain brief information about what you do and why someone should shop at your store. This is a good place to unveil your unique selling proposition. In other words, what do you do or offer that is better than anyone or anything else? For example, with our fictitious *My Fabulous Antique Trains*:

"Welcome to My Fabulous Antique Trains. If you love collecting trains, here is the first stop and last stop you want to make on your journey for additions to your collection. We offer the most extensive, high-quality but low-cost, line of trains. Whether your interest is in a common name brand or the unusual and rare, we are the best place for your online shopping. If you do not

see your item listed here, drop us a line and we will conduct the research for you."

About Us page: On this page, give shoppers a little background and history about your company. You might tell them when and why you opened your store, where you are located, and your philosophy about online shopping. Here is a fictitious example for *My Fabulous Antique Trains.*

"My love affair with antique trains began as a child when I visited the magnificent toy train display at Chicago's Museum of Science and Industry. Since seeing that first train, I have collected and studied antique trains, hoping one day to share my passion with others. The opportunity came to me three years ago when friends encouraged me to open my own online store. The rest, as they say, is history.

Since opening my store, I have expanded into other antique toy niches, including vintage Madame Alexander dolls and wooden toy collections.

At My Fabulous Antique Trains, you will find unusual, one-of-a-kind trains, accessories, and gifts for the train lover. I hope you will enjoy poking around the site. Perhaps you will fall in love with the trains, too. Happy Shopping!"

Privacy page: Yahoo! provides you with standardized text that you can edit as needed.

Copyright page: Here, too, Yahoo! provides you with standardized text that you can edit as needed.

Keep in mind that all your text should be simple and focus on the problem you plan to solve for your customer. Except for the About Us page, where you get to talk a little bit about your company, you want the text to be focused on your customer, not you.

Also, while you should plan your text in advance, you can make changes to it at any time using the Yahoo! Store Editor.

6. Upload changes to the server and select "View Site" to see your store's progress to date. This is just a sneak peak of your site. While you may see the site from this menu item, it is not yet published on the Web. Others cannot see it.

Design Tips

Standard badge
select standard or secure

Monochromatic badge
select standard or secure

Purple badge
select standard or secure

Reproduced with permission of Yahoo! Inc. ® 2009 by Yahoo! Inc. Yahoo! and the Yahoo! Logo are trademarks of Yahoo! Inc

Here are a few pointers to keep in mind when you are designing your Web site:

- **Simple is the key.** You may have plenty of widgets, audio, visual, and flash to put on your Web site, but that does not mean you should use it. The buyer wants to find the items easily and not be bombarded. If people have difficulty getting around your site, they are not going to stick around for long and surely will not come back again. You can always ask your customers to comment on the layout.

- **Keep your links easy to find.** If there is too much going on, it will be difficult for your customers to know how to get to their next destination. Use clear, descriptive text links, even if you have visuals.

- **Put the most important information on the top-left corner of your page**.

- **You never know what page your customers will see first or where they will travel once they get to your Web site.** Be sure that each page has your logo and a navigation bar, so they can get back home. Put a site map in an easily found location, as well. Make it simple to get back home — three clicks at the most.

- **Let your customers/clients know exactly what they have to do to get the information or products they want:** "Sign up here for newsletter." "Sale Items." "Start your order." Then have the link right there.

- **Include a good mix of information and products on your Web site.** People want to learn more about your niche, and the search engines are always looking for valuable information. If you do not have a blog, then be sure to regularly update the information on your Home Page.

- **Make sure the pages open up quickly.** Too many bells and whistles, and it will take too long for the download. Customers do not have patience to wait. They will go right to the next site. This means you should avoid using many large images.

- **Do not use too many colors — two or three complimentary colors at most.** Do not use background colors that make copy difficult to read, such as a black background with a light colored text or yellow and pink type. Use white space to break up the page. Similarly, do not use more than two text fonts, and use the ones that are most common to all browsers.

- **Make sure visitors know that you are a Yahoo! store.** This increases your credibility and decreases concerns about safety.

- **Always include your name and phone number,** so you are a "real person" and customers know how to reach you.

- **Before you go "live," try out your Web site on several different browsers.**

CASE STUDY: SCOTT SMIGLER

Scott Smigler, President
Exclusive Concepts
300 Bear Hill Road
Waltham, MA 02451
1-781-222-1016
www.exclusiveconcepts.com

After getting a basic Yahoo! store up and running, many merchants recognize the need to enhance their Web site to maximize the power of e-commerce and Yahoo!. As with any other product, numerous service providers offer Yahoo! store design and marketing. And, just as with any other product, these online resources vary in experience, results, and quality.

Scott Smigler, president of Exclusive Concepts in Waltham, Massachusetts, agrees that the Yahoo! platform is a good foundation for kicking off the business. Beyond this, however, there is no "one size fits all" when it comes to online merchandising. "The organization of the site and the thought that goes into its content is of critical importance," he explains. "Web design software should not dictate a company's marketing strategy! The message and organization of the Web site must clearly and quickly answer the questions, 'What can you do for me,' 'Why should I care,' and 'How do I contact you,' or the merchant is at an extreme disadvantage." The construction of a truly effective Web site requires human thought to determine an overall design and marketing strategy.

Smigler exemplifies the Netpreneurs who have grown along with online growth. When he was younger, Smigler thought he wanted to be a neurosurgeon, but decided instead to work on computer brains.

CASE STUDY: SCOTT SMIGLER

He started his business while attending high school at the end of the 1990s. By the time he graduated Bentley College, he had helped many clients build successful Web sites, including one that went from zero to $7 million in annual online revenue. He went from being a lone contributor to a staff of 26.

"The organization of the site and the thought that goes into its content is of critical importance."

Today, Exclusive Concepts has established itself as the leading resource for growing stores seeking to convert online shoppers into loyal buyers, specializes in advanced search engine marketing services, and uses an innovative approach to convert Web site browsers into Web site buyers. Smigler's team relies on multivariate testing that analyzes such factors as site layout, messaging, color schemes, and shopping cart usage to determine a store's customer credibility. Such customization, along with tools such as search engine optimization, has increased the growth of many stores by millions of dollars. "We are here to capture extra purchasing power and make the Yahoo! sites leverage their greatest strategic opportunities."

Now, let us get into more depth.

Connecting with Your Customers

The way money is made online involves more than just getting potential customers to your site. It also entails building a relationship with these visitors, so they are encouraged to stay for more than the product and return to your site on a regular basis for what it has to offer. During this time, you are building up your credibility as an expert in the topic of interest associated with the Web site. It is increasingly being noticed in the virtual world that people are craving information and want to spend time with others who share their interests and are knowledgeable about a particular subject. Product, alone, especially when prices among competitors are comparable, does not sell.

If you have a Web site with only products listed, even if you are a retailer, you will not encourage visitors to stay for long or to come back often. Just as important, the site will not do well with the search engines, which are always looking for new content. Unless your product descriptions are different than your competitors', you have the same copy as anyone else. Although it is advisable to set up a blog, you still want your Web site to provide new information and interest visitors. You may conduct an aggressive advertising campaign, implement a multifaceted viral marketing program, and participate in several affiliate programs, but if your Web site does not have interesting copy, you are not going to bring in traffic. Content that gives advice, entertains, informs, and educates can attract and retain visitors and potential customers more than any other promotional tool.

People want to see the same products only so many times, but regularly updating your site's content makes you the knowledgeable source about a topic of interest and gives you a jump over the competition. Customers and new potential buyers will want to come to your site, because they know there is always something of interest when they visit. It is essential that your Web site immediately lets users know they came to the right place for just what they expected. If you can meet your visitors' needs, then display this information clearly and concisely on all your Web site pages.

On the Web site, it is important to 1) display and sell your items or services, 2) grow a niche community and build traffic, and 3) increase the search engine optimization ranking. Placing SEO keywords into the new copy should be done on all your Web pages — and the more pages you have with solid content, the better the results will be. You also should be distinctly defining your company and its product line on each page, since visitors can end up arriving at any page on your site. The Internet is not straightforward, like reading a book with a beginning and end. Also remember that on a Web site, users can travel in many different directions. Unless you redirect them to your home page, they may never get there to buy your products, or even know the name of the company that is offering such interesting information.

At the very least, have a simple header and footer on each page, with a menu and links to additional pages. You should also have a brief paragraph at the top left corner of each page, the most read location, to give the reader a better understanding of where he or she ended up. What Web site is associated with this page? What information, products, or services can you find here? How does the visitor get back home? This not only helps the searcher know what to expect, but it offers additional information for the search engines.

For some Yahoo! store owners, the technical part of this business is a breeze, but the editorial part is torture. When asked to write one or two articles a week, they cringe. You are not being asked to write a bestselling novel. You just have to write about the product or industry you know best. If it is difficult for you to write, then jot down your ideas and have someone you know flush the article out. It is only 200 to 300 words — not even a full page of double-spaced copy — that will feed the search engines each week once you get going.

Then you need to add your keywords to the copy and the title. Since your keywords are about your product, this will not be difficult. If I am writing about a toy locomotive that I just saw at an auction that went for twice the amount expected, I will use the keywords in my copy several times without even trying. Just remember not to go overboard with these keywords. I am not writing, "The toy locomotive auction sold toy locomotives and one toy locomotive sold for much more than most toy locomotives do!"

The following are different ideas for adding either to your home page or to the other pages attached to your Web site. Of course, you do not want to include all these on your home page. Yet, in follow-up pages, you are able to offer the readers a good deal of more solid material. If you have a blog, remember to include an updated notice to let visitors know they can find other information on this topic, along with a link. Include a Table of Contents on your home page with the information available on other pages and a link to a site map. People look for information in different ways.

Voice Your Own Thoughts

You can say whatever you want about your topic, as long as you do not offend your readers. But, sometimes, that works as well. You want them to see you as a person who has considerable knowledge to share, not only on toy locomotives, but also on antique art, and perhaps music. You know your audience, so you know the topics that will interest them. If you want to be sure, just ask them. Most people online are not shy. They will write in and let you know about topics of interest. If your buyers respect your input about the products you sell, they will likely want to hear about your other thoughts as well.

What Do Your Visitors Think?

You want to encourage other people to write in. This means that you are making them think enough about your comments that they want to respond. It will get others to reply to what they have said. This is the way that forums get started. Over time, you become known as an expert and can also evaluate other Web sites and Internet resources, such as e-books and e-zine articles. This interaction with your visitors establishes closer relationships, helps you better understand their needs and interests, gives them a means for addressing suggestions and complaints, provides an avenue for feedback on your products and services, and assists in building a loyal community. At the same time, you are getting fresh, new content for your site that both the visitors and search engines love.

Visitors like to voice their own opinions. Find different ways to encourage people to express themselves or to let you know they have stopped by. You can take a poll or survey, for example, on a specific product or topic of interest that has to do with your theme.

For example, if you sell garden supplies, you can ask visitors to let others know how they are saving money or doing their share to make the world more green. If you sell kitchen items, you can ask for suggestions on ways to still buy enjoyable foods that are becoming pricey in the stores. A survey is another way of gaining input. It need be no longer than eight questions, with "yes" and "no" responses. This can give you more information about your visitors' demographics. Offer a discount or free e-book to those who participate. This is also another way to generate names for e-zines and e-mails. Just make sure that people agree, or "opt in," to this service.

You can also ask your customers for comments on your business and Web site. What do they like or not like? What would they change? What suggestions do they have for other information? How was their buying experience? Be sure to provide an over-view of results, if you decide to go this route. Your readers will want to know how others think.

Asking for Feedback

It is important to have a noticeable place on your Web site that is always asking for feedback on the layout and design, prod-ucts, and content. You always want to hear from your customers and other visitors. The more they feel a part of your Web site, the more they will be encouraged to buy and tell others about you. Today, "others" can be thousands of people through forums, blogs, and social sites. It is not as if they are only communicat-ing with one or two people down the street. If a business scams a customer, you can bet that it will be on Google in a very short time. News travels fast, especially negative news. Getting feed-back also gives you a better indication of whether your products meet the populations' needs or have to be altered. For example, if you are getting mostly teenagers to your Web site, you may want to add products that are more geared toward younger consumers or highlight those that you already sell for that age group.

Your visitors also like to hear from one another, as they become part of a community of people who have similar interests. On every page, offer a link for an e-mail address or feedback form to let visitors write in with their comments, opinions, and suggestions. You should also noticeably display the company's full name, phone number, physical location, and fax number. Some e-commerce sites only include an e-mail or, even less, an e-mail form. As online consumers have become savvier, they are starting to shy away from those Web sites that do not provide specific contact information.

Including "About" Us Information

Similarly, people want to know about your business. With so much fraud and many concerns about safety online, your customers want to know that they are buying from a reputable company. This is especially true if your items are costly. How do they know you offer a reliable service and provide quality product for their money if they do not know anything about you? Being associated with Yahoo! is a big plus for credibility. Yet, more references are needed. People want input. Who are you? What products do you sell? How many years have you been in business? Why should they purchase an item from you instead of the hundreds of other vendors who sell similar merchandise? What are your quality standards? What features and benefits do you offer? How do you rate with your customers?

That is why testimonials and the Yahoo! rating system are so important. If your customers or clients are saying good things about you, let everyone know. You do not want to brag about it on the home page, but your inner pages can include testimonials from users. Prospective customers who are making a buying decision should be able to find all the facts they need to make that choice without having to call or e-mail you for more information.

Come to the Source for More Information

Your visitors want to build up their knowledge base. You can provide that service, rather than having them go to another location. In this case, you do not have to write anything, because plenty of other people already have. Offer a library of articles of interest, in addition to your own blog and newsletter articles. If you are keeping up with the latest updates on your products or your industry in general, you probably read a number of items of interest. There always seems to be something controversial or of note going on. Do not provide a link to those articles, as you do not want to lose your potential customers as they wander off to another site. Rather, copy these materials right into your library, and give credit to the source. Always let the sources know that you are adding their information to your Web site. Reciprocity is a good way to let people on other sites know about your products. You should be making a list of other blogs and Web sites that offer similar or related products to yours. If you need ideas, just visit some sites yourself. You will have to devote a couple of hours each day to marketing.

The Whole FAQs

A Frequently Asked Questions (FAQs) page can provide information to your visitors, build trust, and keep you from getting the same questions repeatedly. Even if you do get an e-mail on the subject, you can respond by giving the link for additional information. The FAQs should, at minimum, help visitors learn more about products that are listed, explain how to order products, provide information on shipping and days to receipt, give an overview of the refund policy, tell how to give feedback for a product and service, and explain how to reach the company. Depending on your Web site and other communications and offerings, such as blogs, e-zines, e-mails, and special bonuses, your FAQs will have different questions and answers. When you write the page, put on your "customer hat," so you can cover as much needed information as possible. Also, the FAQs are similar to the site map, in that they can be picked up by the search engines. This is especially true if you have just introduced a new product that has not yet received much coverage.

Testimonials and Positive Comments

Include testimonials and positive feedback from customers. You do not want to flaunt them, but from time to time, you will receive an e-mail from a customer who is pleased with your service and/or products. E-mail the person back with a "thank you" and ask whether the comments can be made public with/without a name. Also, whenever another media, such as a Web site or newspaper, mentions your company, especially for an award or honor, be sure to highlight that on your home page.

Clean, Easily Readable Design

Web site visitors like pages that are clean, clear, and easy-to-read and navigate. It is all right to use widgets or other design elements to spark up your page, but too many bells and whistles make readers disinterested. Grammatical and spelling errors on Web sites reflect the quality of your products, and poor Web design does the same. When the Web first started, everyone's page looked the same, with straight copy and a variety of colors. Then, when new design elements came in, such as animated gifs, audio, and video, there were numerous pages that were weighed down with too many extras. It is amazing how many Web sites continue to have words that are misspelled, horrible grammar, and a complete mess of visuals, so you cannot find anything. It is much better to put fewer items on a page that are easy to see and pleasing to the eye than to try to pack so much information that it is difficult to finding anything.

The best approach is moderation. Since your buyers like pages that download quickly with easy-to-find, relevant copy, decide on a good middle ground between too much and too little copy and design. Just as in print, white space is important in Web design. You do not want to cram too much onto a page or have such small type that it is barely readable. You also want the visitors to find the Table of Contents easily. Yet, you do not want links on the top, sides, and bottom of each page. Two places for this information are helpful. Seeing a design that works well at one Web site does not mean that it will be just as effective for yours. As with your Web site copy, you need to know what is best for your visitors. You can also run surveys about your design, similar to those mentioned for Web site copy, to see whether you are meeting your users' visual needs and interests.

Becoming a Part of the Virtual Community

The Internet is just one massive universe of smaller communities.

People may be from anywhere in the world and have completely different backgrounds, but they will find others that have similar views and interests. For many people, it is easier to find like individuals online than in their own offline world. To be successful with your Yahoo! site, you need to establish yourself as a part of this community and as an expert in a particular area that is in line with the products you sell.

Copywriting Suggestions

You do not need to hire a professional copywriter to have a good Web site, but you should keep these guidelines in mind when you write text for your Yahoo! store.

- **Use easy-to-understand language.** People are shopping, not reading a novel, so text should be simple to understand, concise, and easy to read. Sixth-grade level is ideal, unless all your readers have a specialty in English grammar or physics.

- **Get right to the point.** Use as few words as possible to convey your message. You want to fill up space, but being repetitive will not be any better than writing nothing at all.

- **Do not forget those keywords.** Keep a list of your top 100 keywords by you when writing. Use as many of these SEO words on your site as possible, including keywords in the titles, section heads, and product pages. By using keywords in critical areas of your site (e.g., page title and title tags), search engines are more likely to rank you favorably. However, do not overload your page with these keywords. Neither the customers nor the search engines like "Buy your dog bones at the dog bone store."

- **Ensure that your text is error free.** Nothing turns off a shopper like typos. The rationale? If you cannot spell correctly, what else are you doing wrong? Use your computer's spell-check and grammar check tools and have at least one other person proofread your copy before posting it to your Web store.

- **Update your text frequently.** Shoppers like to think that the online stores where they shop regularly update their sites. Keep your home page text fresh by noting changes to the site, new product lines, and special promotions. Consider adding a "What's New" page or section somewhere on your site for easy locating. The search engines love updated copy. It is the best way to get high rankings.

- **Add customer testimonials.** Shoppers are more likely to believe a customer testimonial than they are to believe your marketing lingo about your latest product. Solicit customer feedback by thanking them for their purchase, asking whether they have questions, and requesting feedback on what they liked about their shopping experience (e.g., quality of product, affordability, shipping options, and customer service). Before posting testimonials to your Yahoo! store, however, make sure you get permission from the shopper. If possible, get a photo of him or her with the new purchase and post it alongside the testimonial. It creates a good visual for prospective customers.

CASE STUDY: MATT SAMPSON

Matt Sampson, CEO
Colorado Web Solutions
8302 Beech Street
Arvada, CO 80005
1-888- 501-5550
www.coloradowebsolutions.com

"Of course you want to list your products and prices, but the stores that are going to succeed have great content and change it all the time."

Many merchants who sign up with a Yahoo! store find the site's template meets their needs. They get it up and running and tweak it as necessary. Other store owners want their site to look different than the norm or to have additional technical features. In such cases, they turn to organizations such as Colorado Web Solutions in Arvada, Colorado.

CEO Matt Sampson knows Yahoo! inside and out; he has been working with Yahoo! stores since 1997 when a company called ViaWeb owned the technology. About 99.9 percent of Colorado Web Solutions' clients are Yahoo! store owners — some new and others already established. "Businesses do not need a formal strategy when calling us," explains Sampson, "but they need to seriously consider what they are selling, where they are going to get this product and, most importantly, who their audience is." In other words, too often, merchants open a store because they are interested in a product line, but they have not given nearly enough thought to the specific market. It is certainly important that sellers like the merchandise or services they offer, but they need to know it fills a need.

CASE STUDY: MATT SAMPSON

Another mistake Yahoo! store owners frequently make, notes Sampson, is forgetting the importance of content. "Of course you want to list your products and prices," he explains, "but the stores that are going to succeed have great content and change it all the time. Instead of using just the manufacturer's description for a product, write your own details as well. Create a feel for your audience by offering content found nowhere else, but also attract the search engines with your own unique content. It's those descriptions that you write that will bring in your first customers. Customers who will trust you based on what you say. It just grows from there."

Sampson says that his business continues to grow along with the increasing number of Yahoo! e-merchants who need Web design, search engine optimization support, and other marketing tools, such as blogs and e-mail marketing. He has expanded from a 200-square-foot room, when he first started the company, to nearly 20 employees worldwide, and he continues to set his sights (or sites) as high as those Colorado mountains.

CHAPTER 9

Put Up Your Storefront, Part 2

N ow that you have the design and copy completed, it is time to get to your products. This is the part that many enjoy more than anything, while others find it long and tedious. That is what a business is all about — many different responsibilities with many different hats.

Adding Products

With Yahoo! Merchant Solutions store builder, you can upload product images, descriptions, and pricing information. Materials required: digital photos/images of your products, descriptions, names, and prices. Yahoo! recommends that you allocate about five minutes per item you will be adding, if you use Yahoo!'s Add Product Wizard. We recommend ten minutes, particularly as you learn to use the system. To begin, click on "Start Adding Products." This often is the most time-consuming part of the layout, especially if you have hundreds of items. Set aside some time every day to for adding items.

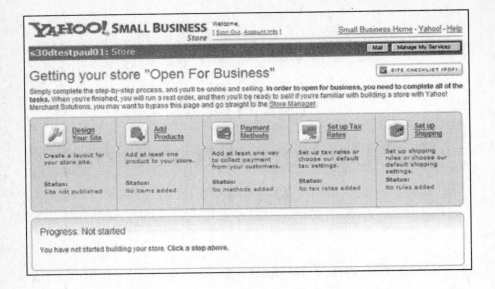

*Note: Advanced users can upload their data in batches using a file with a *.csv format. Merchants creating their own site with tools other than Yahoo!'s Site Builder will be taken to the Catalog Manager to upload product information.

Reproduced with permission of Yahoo! Inc. ® 2009 by Yahoo! Inc. Yahoo! and the Yahoo! Logo are trademarks of Yahoo! Inc

1. Enter product information. You will complete the following information:

   • Product name — The name should be brief but explanatory.

   • Detailed description — Describe your product from a customer's perspective. If you were buying the product, what would you want to know about it? Size? Dimensions? Color? Features? Functionality? Material? Specifications?

   • Product images — Select an appropriate digital image of your product. Such images are most likely available from your suppliers. Ask for Web-friendly images you can use on your site and request written permission to post them online. If you are securing your own products or making them yourself, you can take your own digital photos. If you are offering services rather than products, search for appropriate photos or representative images online. If you use stock photography or online clip art, make sure you obtain permission to re-use the image on a commercial site.

- Price — Identify the price point for each product.

- Sales price — Add a sales price, if applicable.

- Ship-weight — Indicate the product's shipping weight, if applicable.

- Mark product as "special" — If you check this box for a given product, it will appear on your store's home page. This is a good option, especially for sale, clearance, or seasonal items.

After entering each product, Yahoo! will ask whether you want to Create Options for that product. If so, click "Yes" and proceed to the next screen to add the pertinent information. If not, click "No" and continue.

Repeat the above process for each product. Rest assured that even if you are not computer savvy, the onscreen instructions are easy to follow.

2. When you have input all your products, Yahoo! will ask you to assign each product to a category. You can create

product categories to further organize items in your store. For example, if you sell clothing, you might break your products down into men's, women's, children's, and uni-sex clothing. You might add a category for accessories or sale items. If you offer both products and services, you might separate your offerings by having a products cat-egory and a services category.

3. Review your newly created products/categories and make any necessary changes.

4. Yahoo! will give you the option of creating additional products, following the same process as above. If you are done entering product information, select "Finish."

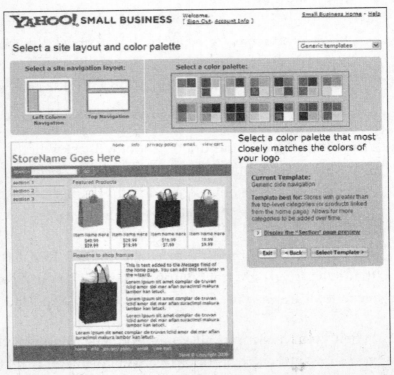

Click the **Insert Image** button on your editing toolbar.

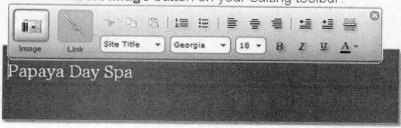

In the **Add an Image** dialog, click the **Browse** button.

In the **Add an Image** dialog, you'll see some information in the **Image** field. This is the "address," or path, to your image. Click **Add Image** to insert the image in your site title.

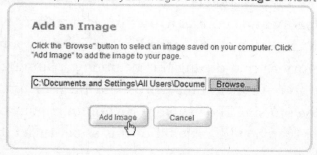

8. Click the **Save** button to save your changes.

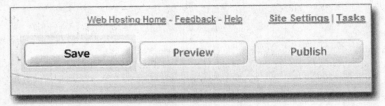

Your logo will now appear on every page of your site.

Hint: Is your logo too big? Resize it by dragging the corners of the image.

Reproduced with permission of Yahoo! Inc. ® 2009 by Yahoo! Inc. Yahoo! and the
Yahoo! Logo are trademarks of Yahoo! Inc

Writing Catalog Copy

Your catalog copy is just as important as the copy on your Web site or blog. In addition to selling products, it can also be used as a means to increase ranking in the search engines and to encourage new customers to buy. Develop an outline for your catalog that includes categories and sub categories. You may want to consult with a search engine optimization specialist who can help you leverage your catalog as much as possible to grow sales. It is essential to have your category and product names relate to concepts for which people search. You need to carefully think about your navigation and category format during this beginning planning stage to ensure that you are including words and phrases that can generate traffic to your site. The keywords in your navigation system are crucial for search engine visibility. It is easier to get it right the first time than to go back later and rewrite the copy.

Then, again, you do not have to add 50,000 items right away. It is better to have a well-defined, usable catalog with fewer items than a huge one that is less user-friendly. Getting the keywords in the works as soon as possible is important so you can begin to bring people to your site. Being recognized by the search engines does not occur over night. It is better having a Web site go up with a few dozen products than waiting half a year to get 500 products listed.

Remember that all of this copy has to be original. You cannot recreate copy that you have received from your manufacturers that other sites are using or cut and paste from another site. Google frowns on such duplication and will drop you because of it. Google only displays the first page it indexes with that same content. Expect to have to write your own quality, keyword-rich category and product descriptions. This takes more time for merchants than most other responsibilities.

If you are competing with several other sites that are all getting their products and content from the same manufacturer, your site will stand out from the pack in the Google rankings if you include unique content. There are many places online where you can get someone to write catalog copy for you at a reasonable rate. Just do not go too low in your rates paid, since you will attract more beginning writers and will have to edit the material.

Similarly, if you want to sell your merchandise online, you must have high-quality photographs for each product, as well as supporting documentation, when possible, such as brochures, specification sheets, instructions, and user manuals. These documents will convert interest into sales and will be used for search engine traffic. Develop a clear, easy-to-read catalog look to convert sales. Large, bold fonts with loud colors or ugly buttons will not attract viewers.

Cross-selling and Up-selling features

"Popular products," "related products," and "also purchased" are the names of popular up-selling and cross-selling vehicles. The idea is to show your site visitors those other products that they might be interested in purchasing. If they are looking at a pair of slacks, show them a matching blouse/shirt and jacket. It is well worth your time to find some of these connections and point them out to your potential buyers.

Search Engine Considerations

It is important for search engine visibility to have keyword-rich product categories listed in your catalog. Also consider developing good short and long category descriptions, as well as short and long product descriptions. Often, with online catalogs, the buyer clicks from the home to a category page, which only has links to other product pages, plus a couple of pictures. This is a major SEO advantage lost. Think of all the key phrases you can have when describing your products, which can be picked up by the search engines. Because category pages only display items in a specific category, they are perfect stages for SEO keywords.

For example, suppose you have a site that sells Gucci products. You can have categories such as Gucci handbags, Gucci jewelry, and Gucci wallets. You can also have a brief, keyword-filled description of each listing and then additional text on each product page. Depending on your product, you will also want to add technical information on the product description page. By leveraging your Web catalog copywriting, you can get your e-commerce site ranked highly in the search engines, and customers and higher sales will follow. Hire an SEO firm to research traffic patterns and degrees of competition for relevant search phrases. Be aware that not all SEO consultants are created equal. Some swear they can get you number-one rankings all the time, but do not believe it. Go with the one who says that they will get high rankings, but that those rankings will continually change. Also check out the firm's credentials with others.

All Avenues Possible

When browsing your Yahoo! store, shoppers can use two senses — sight and sound — and you should leverage both opportunities. Make your store visually appealing with crisp, clear photos and graphics, and when appropriate, you can use audio clips that describe your products, have customer testimonials, or even something of general interest. Explain how your product or service can save time or money or solve a personal problem. If you engage your customers in the online shopping experience at your Yahoo! store, they are more likely to remember it for future purchases and recommend you to friends. They will also keep coming back.

Remember that you can cross-sell your items in Yahoo! Shopping, which holds one of the top market shares in the shopping search business. Through your Store Manager "product submit," you can have your merchandise information put directly on Yahoo! Shopping. Because of your Yahoo! affiliation, customers get a 20 percent discount off the rate. You can also pay a cost-per-click fee for each visitor. How successful you are at selling is largely based on how your products appeal to the customers, the amount of competition, and how well you optimize your product listings. Shopping search results depend on product relevancy and your customer ratings.

Setting Up Payment Options

Yahoo! allows you to accept multiple options for payment. If you already have a merchant account, contact Yahoo! to determine whether it is compatible with the existing system. If you do not have a merchant account already, Yahoo! offers several options. Either you can apply for an account with PayPal or First Data, or you can use your own if you have a premier or business account with another firm.

- Select "Set Up My First Payment Method." Yahoo! will ask: "Are you currently able to accept payments through credit cards or PayPal?" You have two choices. "No, I need to sign up for a payment processing method," or "Yes, I am currently able to accept and process payments." Choose the appropriate answer.

- If you selected "No," you will be asked what type of online payment method you would like to set up. The first choice (1) is "Accept Credit Cards Directly on My Web site with a Merchant Account." You can then select to apply for an account with PayPal.

- The second choice (2) is to accept credit card and PayPal payments on the PayPal Web site using PayPal's Express Checkout service. The latter choice is recommended for newer merchants who need an easy way to accept payments. There are no monthly fees or approval processes.

- If you selected (2), you will have three choices: (a) "I want to configure my store using my current PayPal account" [Note: Your PayPal account must be a PayPal Premier or Business account to qualify.]; (b) "I want to configure my store to use my existing business account from my merchant account." This assumes your existing merchant account is compatible with the FDMS Nashville platform to process payments online; or (c) "I want to configure my store to process payments offline." Option (c) is not recommended by Yahoo! and may turn away potential customers. The goal of having an online store is to be able to make purchases and process orders online. Choosing this option defeats that purpose, creating more work for you.

- If you selected (2a), Yahoo! takes you to a screen where you can configure your PayPal account. Click on "Configure PayPal" to be taken to the PayPal login.

Setting up a merchant account

Ask your merchant account provider for a new MID/TID pair for your Yahoo! Store. You should ask them to use the following information in the setup:

- Product Name: Yahoo! Store FDMS (g/w)
- Product ID:819000
- Vendor Name: Yahoo!
- Vendor ID:190

Once you have this information, you will need to sign in to your store to set up online processing.

To set up an existing merchant account:

1. From Store Manager, click the "Payment Center" link under the "Order Settings" column. (You may be prompted to enter your security key to proceed).
2. Click **Add New Processor**.
3. Select the option to use your **existing payment processor**.
4. Select the option to **configure an existing merchant account** and click **Next**.
5. Enter your merchant account information supplied to you by your merchant account provider into the fields and select the supported credit cards (see A-D Figure 1):

Notes about multiple merchant accounts

- Merchants with multiple merchant accounts can switch which account through which to process a manual transaction by selecting the account using the gateway drop-down menu on the Manual Transactions page. The gateway field will appear at the top of the fields in the Submit and Void Transactions sections.
- Each merchant account should be set to process a unique set of card types (Visa, MasterCard) without overlapping.
- Merchants cannot use the authorization from one merchant account to process a manual transaction in another merchant account.
- Merchants should check with their merchant account providers to determine what circumstances result in non-qualified transactions so as to avoid the higher fees typically associated with such transactions.

YAHOO! SMALL BUSINESS   Welcome, pboisvert04
[Sign Out, Account Info]   Small Business Home · Help

Enter your existing Merchant Account information

Use the fields below to set up your merchant account to process credit cards online through FDMS, the Yahoo! Store Payment Processor.
If you have an existing merchant account, you will need to request a new MID (merchant identification) and TID (terminal identification) for
use with Yahoo! Store using the information in the box below.

Note: Your merchant account must be compatible with FDMS Nashville in order to process transactions online. Contact your merchant
account provider to determine if your account is compatible. If your account is not compatible, you can choose to sign up with Paymentech,
PayPal, or a compatible provider, or you can choose to process transactions offline.

Name of Bank [   ] — A

Merchant Number [   ] — B
    For your reference only -- not used
    by the software.

MID (Merchant Identification) [   ] — C
    Check this number carefully. You
    can omit leading zeros.

TID (Terminal Identification) [   ] — D
    Check this number carefully. You
    can omit leading zeros.

You may need to provide the following
information to your bank:
  • ProductName: Yahoo! Store FDMS (g/w)
  • Product ID: 819000
  • Vendor Name: Yahoo!
  • Vendor ID: 190

[Exit] [< Back] [Finish]

Copyright © 2007 Yahoo! Inc. All rights reserved.
Privacy Policy - Copyright Policy - Terms of Service - Help

Figure 1: Setting up an existing merchant account

Setting Up Taxes

Before setting up tax rates in your Yahoo! store, contact a local taxing authority or financial expert (e.g., government, chamber of commerce, merchants association, state attorney general, bookkeeper, or accountant) to find out what the applicable laws are in your jurisdiction. Tax laws may vary by state, county, and city; contact the necessary taxing entities to cover all your bases.

In particular, find out whether you are required to collect sales tax on in-state and out-of-state purchases. If so, find out the current tax rates for those jurisdictions and get instructions on how to submit those taxes to the appropriate taxing authority. You only need the tax rate information to set up your Yahoo! store, but you will need the other information to manage the daily operations of your business.

1. Click on "Start Tax Wizard."

2. Answer this question: "Are you required to collect tax online?" Your options are: "I am not required to collect tax" (applicable for service businesses); "I am required to collect tax on taxable goods purchased from my online store;" and "I am not sure if I am required to collect taxes."

Setting Up Shipping

1. To set up shipping options for your Yahoo! store, click on "Start Shipping Wizard." Yahoo! estimates time spent on this task at 15 minutes. Required materials: where you will be shipping from, who you will be shipping to (e.g., United States only, United States and Canada, or internationally), and what shippers you would like to use.

2. Yahoo! will first ask you how you want to set up rates. Do you want to use UPS' Real Time Rates system (This Yahoo!-recommended option will require a UPS account), manually enter your own rates, or, if you are not sure, select "I'm not sure how I want to set up shipping rates."

3. Select your Yahoo! store in the list provided. If you only have one store, only one option will appear. Click "Continue."

4. If you chose UPS Real Time Rates, you will enter your UPS

account information. If you selected to enter your own rates manually, you will get a list of other shipping options from which to choose. Select those options that you wish to offer (e.g., UPS ground, FedEx ground, and UPS two-day air), and set up your own rates. You can set up a rate table by item count, cost, weight, or any other criteria you determine. As an alternative, you can choose a flat rate for each type of service. If you are not sure what options you want to offer or what rates you should charge, Yahoo! will direct you to the vendors' Web sites for more information. Follow the on-screen instructions.

Open for Business

When working on your store, Yahoo! will let you know when you have completed all the required steps before publishing it to the Web. Next, Yahoo! recommends that you place a test order before going live. This will help you understand your customer's experience firsthand.

Placing a test order

1. Go to your store's URL.

2. Review your store's products and select one to purchase.

3. Choose an item and select "Add to Cart."

4. Go through the checkout process as if you were buying the item. Try using a valid credit card for your purchase to be sure your payment is processed correctly.

5. Did everything go smoothly? Did you have any questions

that were not answered on-screen?

Now we will log into your Yahoo! account and view the order to see whether it was processed correctly.

1. Log into your account.

2. Go to the "Store Control Panel."

3. From the Process menu, select "Orders." A red asterisk (*) should appear if a new order is pending.

4. Select your order and review it for accuracy.

5. Cancel the order when you are finished reviewing it, so Yahoo! does not charge you transaction fees for the mock purchase.

Now you can publish your Web site, if you are all set with the way it looks. Hit the "Publish" button, and you are all set to go.

Control Panels for Easy-to-Make Store Changes

O nce you have opened your Yahoo! store, you can still make changes to it. Simply log into your Small Business account and click "Store Editor" from the menu (far left side of your screen). Click on the Web page you want to update, and select "Edit" from the menu at the top of the screen. If you want to update your Home page text, for example, click on the "Home" page and then click "Edit." Make the desired changes, and then update. Unlike making changes to Web site coding, editing a Yahoo! store is fairly simple. Just edit your pages and upload the changes to your Web store by clicking on "Publish Order Settings" at the bottom of the fourth column.

1. Log into Yahoo! Merchant Solutions

2. Go to Store Manager

3. Go to Store Editor or Store Control Panel

Store Editor Control Panel

Before we let you explore the Store Editor on your own, we will provide you with a brief tutorial on what you need to know about making edits and changes to your site.

Home Page Menu Bar

This feature allows you to perform a multitude of editing functions on your Web site. The top menu bar includes a number of different commands. Your most-used key will be "Edit."

Let us go through each feature to see what it does. Per Yahoo!'s Help file, the commands do the following:

Edit: Allows you to edit properties for the Index (Home) page.

Edit All: Allows you to edit all the points from this point down.

Section: Allows you to create a new section and list it here.

Item: Allows you to create a new item and list it here.

Link: Allows you to create an external link and list it here.

Move: Allows you to drag and drop an item from one location on the site to another.

Image: Allows you to upload a logo.

Look: Allows you to change the background of your store.

Layout: Allows you to change the appearance of your store.

Help/Hide Help: Lets you view instructions for all areas.

Variables: Allows you to change the overall properties of the site, including colors, fonts, page properties, page layouts, headers, and so on.

Manager: Returns you to the Store Manager.

Publish: Writes a copy of your Web site to a specified location. Use this command when you are done editing your site to ensure that changes are posted to the Web.

Red Arrow: Moves you from the Beginner to Advance mode. (If you toggle back and forth on this arrow, you will find that you will/will not see areas in the "Edit" and "Items" section. To see everything, you have to return to the Advance mode.

Find: Helps you locate an item or section based on ID. Every item in your store will have an ID and name which may/may not be the same.

Contents: Takes you to every document, section, and informational page included in the site.

Files: Allows you to upload images you want, such as "Free Shipping."

C4-page: Custom Templates.

Types: Tells you about the Built-In or Custom Type.

Database Upload: Allows you to upload products from a drop-shipper.

Configure: Allows you to set properties for the Store Editor, including the Editor toolbar location, default templates, and other default items.

Controls: Allows you to set Store Editor properties, such as mode and editor entry page, or to access advanced features, such as search, multiple image upload, edit multiple items, and RTML documentation.

When you click the "Edit" button, across the top of the page you will find the:

Edit Menu Bar:

Under this, you will find several more buttons:

Update: Do not confuse the "Update" with the "Publish" button. Both can save the work you have done. However, the "Update" button only saves the work you have done on that one page and does not present the page for all viewers to see. You need to hit the "Publish" button for all your work to be seen by the "external" world. Hit this only when you are set with everything you have done.

Cancel: If you make a mistake and need to re-input, do not worry. Just hit "Cancel."

New Property: Use this if you want to add copy that is not part of the regular template. Once you add copy, it will say "Remove Property." (Be sure to click on the "+" sign by "Custom Property" at the top of the bar. When the "–" sign is there, all the custom copy becomes visible.)

Override Variable: This lets you change the existing block in the object properties. Most variables are set to be the same for each page. If, for example, you have products showing up in three columns, and you want to show them on two columns on one page, just click the "Override Variable" and "Columns." Then click "Update," and make your change.

Remove Property: Here you can eliminate any additional properties you have put in. It will no longer show up as "Custom Property."

Manager: If you want to get back out of the Editor mode, just click this to get to areas such as "Design Wizard," "Catalog Manager," and "Orders."

Section/Item Menu Bar

Under this, you will find several other buttons:

Up: Returns to previous page.

Special: Takes something and duplicates it on the Home Page under Featured Products.

Cut: Eliminates a section you want to move from one area to another and stores it in "Clipboard."

Copy: Duplicates a section.

Delete: Be careful. This will delete an entire ID if you are not on the particular page on which you want it deleted. It will give you a warning, just in case.

For the most part, the features are easy to use. Be careful when making changes, though. If you do not know what you are doing or changing, stop and ask for help. Otherwise, you may be posting unintended changes to your Yahoo! store.

Catalog Manager

The Catalog Manager is a powerful Yahoo! tool that allows you to manage catalog items (add, edit, or delete); manage tables (group items together, edit, or delete groups); track inventory; upload items; create and manage gift certificates (standard and professional packages only); and finally, publish your changes to the Web. This is a dynamic tool with too many capabilities to list here.

Statistics

In the Statistics column, Yahoo! returns a variety of stats you can use to manage your online store. These are quite helpful for you when determining your product mix and how to post products to your Web site. The more you know about your users, the better you can respond to their needs "before" they even arise. You do not want to get into the habit of changing well after a trend has started. In the Internet world, things change so rapidly that you have to keep several steps ahead. Making money means having more than one jump on the competition and constantly considering continuous improvement measures. Selections in the statistics section include:

Page Views: This tool shows income generated from each page of your Web site. Initially, it points out the most popular pages, sorted by number of page views, for the last year. In each line, a thumbnail graph depicts the trend over that period for each page. These graphs can be used to alert you when individual pages become stale. At the bottom of the page, you can change the time period and sort the data. To see what pages are selling best, change the "Sort" criterion to "By Revenue," and click "Show."

Sales: This answers questions about which products are selling the most or generating the most revenue and which products appear in the greatest number of orders. To find out, analyze your site performance for "Count of Items Sold," "Count of Orders," and "Revenue."

References: Here you can see where your visitors came from and how much money people coming from each place spend. Initially, you will see the entries sorted by visitors for the last year, with thumbnail graphs of the trend over time for each referrer. Similar to "Page Views," you can change the time period and sort criteria at the bottom of the page.

For many sites, including search engines, you will see a "Details" link at the end of the line, which will show you detailed data for visitors from that site. For search engines, you should see the actual search keywords your visitors have used and how much money they spent using each keyword. To see which keywords generated the most sales, scroll down to the bottom of the page and change the "Sort" criterion to "By Revenue." For keywords associated with orders, the number in the "Orders" column is a link to the orders placed by customers who searched for that keyword. On average, you will get referrer data for about half your visitors, which tends to be enough to be statistically significant.

Searches: This shows you how visitors to your site have

searched, which helps you better understand your customers and where your site can be improved. When visitors do searches, it often means either that your site is missing something they expect or that some part of your site is too hard to find.

Graphs: Here you can make charts of overall trends in your site for a number of measures and a range of time periods. Initially, it shows you page views for up to the last year, and the options at the bottom of the page let you choose a number of statistics to view. The most important graphs are page views and income, as well as income per page view, because an increase shows that visitors are increasingly confident about ordering from you, and page views per visit, since a decrease means that your site is getting stale.

Click Trails: Look at this statistic to find the paths individual visitors take through your site. This should give you an idea of how your site looks through the customers' eyes. The paths of visitors who put items in the shopping basket can be most informative. You can also view the click trail of any individual customer by clicking on the "Click Trails" link at the bottom of the page showing their order. While most site statistics are saved for 365 days, click trails are only saved for 5 days. Also, some click trails will be useless, if they are generated by proxy servers or search engine crawlers.

Reports: This generates a table summarizing trends in your site. The data can be exported directly to desktop spreadsheets like Excel by clicking on the link to that effect at the bottom.

Repeats: The link labeled "Repeats" leads to the "Repeat

CHAPTER 10: Control Panels for Easy-to-Make Store Changes

Customer Detector," which groups orders that were probably placed by the same person and lists them by number of orders. This matches orders by looking at the name, credit card number, and e-mail address, allowing you to recognize repeat customers without requiring them to register. It is also useful in detecting fraudulent orders.

Additional Tools from Yahoo!

Store Tag Hub: Store tags are small pieces of HTML code that are inserted into product pages and pull information from your product database so changes to prices or descriptions in your catalog are automatically updated in your Web pages. This requires some knowledge of HTML and additional software.

Once you set up your Catalog Manager, you can use the Store Tag Hub to create special coding to update your item pages automatically whenever you make a change to the Catalog Manager. This section includes a tutorial, store tag wizard, store tag editors, a syntax guide, and sample layouts for item and section modules.

Ratings: This tool allows you to display customer ratings on your site, sorted by date or rating. To turn the feature on, select "Use These Settings." Customers use ratings on many different sites (e.g., eBay and Amazon.com) as a basis for choosing to do business with a particular company or to buy a specific product.
Affiliate program: Yahoo! partners with Commission Junction to offer merchants the opportunity to develop a pay-per-performance affiliate program.

Coupon manager: This tool allows you to create and manage coupons for an amount or percentage off the purchase price of one or more products or free shipping. First, you must decide the offer you want to make and assign it a coupon code. Then set up the coupon parameters, such as minimum purchase, if required; expiration date; target products; and trackable links, if necessary. Once the coupon has been created and the coupon code assigned, this coupon code can be used in the next e-mail newsletter, in Web or print advertising, or it can be sent directly to a specific customer.

One of the best ways to draw people to your online store is to offer coupons. Many people who receive a coupon, by e-mail or through your Web site, will visit your store to redeem their coupon and find additional purchases while they are there. One coupon can bring in several sales you otherwise would never make. Then, once you have this customer, you can continue to follow up, offer more coupons and offers, and keep him or her over the long-term.

Turning new customers into existing customers is an important part of helping your online store thrive and building the business for growing income. Offering coupons can help bring in new customers and help convert them into long-term buyers. With Yahoo! Merchant Solutions, offering coupons is easy, since it is built right into your online store. There is no additional programming; just set up your coupon, distribute it, and use it to make more sales.

Coupons are only a part of the offerings at Yahoo! Merchant Solutions. You can also offer gift certificates, which can be an effective sales tool. One of your existing customers gives a gift certificate to a friend, and that friend comes to your store, makes a purchase, and becomes an ongoing customer. The best part about gift certificates is that you not only gain a new customer, you also make the full sale price of the item and offer your customers something new that they cannot get from many of your competitors, who are not using Yahoo! Merchant Solutions and do not have the ability to easily offer gift certificates.

Create links: Here sellers can create trackable links for special offers. Yahoo!'s link tracker tool allows them to create a special code for each Web site that links to the store. It lets merchants track how many visitors and how many sales have come to them from each referring site. To further expand this opportunity, they can create an Affiliate Program, where they pay a fee or a percentage of sales to referring sites.

Other Available Services

The following services are either available with Standard/Professional or at an additional cost:

E-mail marketing: Clicking on this tool will take you from the Yahoo! Merchant Control Panel to its e-mail marketing partner, Campaigner. Yahoo! store merchants are offered a free trial.

Keyword finder: The keyword finder tool helps sellers identify new keywords that are of interest to customers for finding items that might be sold in the Yahoo! store. This information is particularly useful when using search marketing campaigns and SEO. This page also contains a link that will take merchants to a Promotion and Traffic page, which offers other suggestions for marketing the Yahoo! store.

Mailing lists: This tool allows merchants to create different mailing lists. The tool comes with two initial options to create lists for customers who have ordered before and for those who have requested catalogs. In addition, merchants can create new lists, add and remove names from existing lists, review list memberships, and export the list to Microsoft® Excel® for use in creating mailing labels or a more detailed database. You can use your lists to send targeted e-mails from your Yahoo! e-mail account.

Search Engines

The Yahoo! search engine feature allows you to promote your site on search engines using different methods, including:

Yahoo! Site map: By enabling this feature, the tool will automatically generate a site map containing each page of your store. Each time your site is updated using the Yahoo! Store Editor, the site map will be automatically updated. Yahoo! will submit the site map to Yahoo! Search, Google, and other search engines to assist your site in being indexed.

Product catalog submission: This search engine tool gives you the ability to enable and submit your product catalogs to shopping comparison engines and other third-party sites. When you enable these features, Yahoo! will submit your product catalogs to Google Base and provide access to other sites. Each time you publish updated product catalog information, Yahoo! will update its files and links.

Yahoo! Site Explorer: Using the Yahoo! Site Explorer tool, it is possible to see what information Yahoo! has collected about a site's online presence. Sellers can view what sites and sub-pages Yahoo! Search indexes, track the sites that link into Web pages, and view the most popular pages from any site.

Additional methods for driving traffic: In this section, Yahoo! offers information about search engine marketing and how to optimize Web site pages for better indexing through page titles and meta tags. For computer novices, this might sound intimidating, but Yahoo! does a good job of presenting this information in a way that most users can understand.

Google Site maps: Merchants who want to use Google's Web master tools must first verify their ownership of their Web site.

If this is not enough for search engine opportunities, Yahoo! provides a list of additional resources for the following: SEO, Yahoo! store developers who specialize in SEO, search engine articles in Yahoo! Small Business News and Resources, search engine watch, and SEO chat. What is best about this section is that while it is tied to Yahoo!-friendly resources, Yahoo! offers many options and tools for learning more about SEO. You are limited only by your desire to learn.

Yahoo! Search: In this brief section, Yahoo! points merchants in the direction of other Yahoo!-related free and sponsored search inclusion programs. Merchants can submit their stores to several free sites using Yahoo! tools, or they can opt for various price-per-click options including Sponsored Search, Product Submit, and Travel Submit.

MSN site submission: Surprisingly, Yahoo! also provides a link on this page to let users submit their Web site URL directly to MSN.

Simple promotional e-mail: To make it easier for non-marketers, Yahoo! has created a simple promotional e-mail for merchants to send to family and friends to announce the grand opening of their stores. In a few easy steps, anyone can create an attractive announcement that matches the branding of a Yahoo! store. Simply fill in e-mail addresses, select the products to be displayed, add a coupon, save, preview, and send. This is easy to create and send in a matter of minutes.

Yahoo! Directory: For a few hundred dollars, merchants can submit their listing to the Yahoo! directory. This service provides a seven-day review service for business directory listings. This is a duplication of information included in the Yahoo's Search Engine page above. It is not necessary to duplicate the information, but Yahoo! wants to cover all its bases when spreading the word about your store.

Yahoo! search marketing: Divided into sections, this page repeats material presented in earlier menu items, but it is presented differently. This page is easier to read and understand than some of Yahoo!'s previous references to search marketing. Whether you choose to use any of these features depends on the type of Yahoo! store you have, what products and/or services you are selling, your revenue goals, and your marketing and advertising budget.

Yahoo! Sponsored Search: This section describes how Yahoo!'s pay-per-click online advertising program works. It gives a brief explanation as to why sponsored search advertising is important, explains the cost of such a program ($30 minimum deposit), and offers a link and a toll-free phone number for more information.

Yahoo! Shopping: This link takes you to Yahoo!'s Product Submit, where, after updating your product catalog, you can submit your products for inclusion in Yahoo! Shopping, Yahoo! Product Search, and buyer's guide pages. As this is a pay-per-performance program, merchants are charged only when someone clicks on a link and visits their store. Ranging from 12 to 80 cents per click, pricing varies based on the product category.

Keyword search for marketing campaigns: Here Yahoo! directs merchants to a keyword finder tool to help them increase referrals and revenue.

Conversion tracking and reporting: This Yahoo! tool measures the effectiveness of your Yahoo! Search marketing campaigns. This will help you to measure your return on investment (ROI) and will aid in future marketing and budgeting decisions.

Merchant resources

This section includes numerous resources for merchants in the following categories:

Updates: This section includes information on system status, Yahoo! servers, and e-commerce. It also offers a small business newsletter to help merchants promote their products and services online.

Related Services: This section includes additional links to resources listed elsewhere, including links to professional Web site designers who specialize in creating Yahoo! stores, and to Yahoo! Product Submit.

Learn More: In this section, merchants can review additional information about topics they will access frequently. It includes a getting started overview; a downloadable getting started guide; store help; and customer care, credit cards, and Yahoo! store guidelines.

Partners: This section lists some of Yahoo!'s preferred business partners.

Application Notes: This section contains information about other applications that integrate with Yahoo! stores.

System status: The Yahoo! Merchant Solutions System Status allows merchants to see the status of Yahoo! system updates, security updates, solutions in process, and closed work orders. If a merchant notices his or her e-mail is slow, for example, it is possible to check this link to see whether a problem has been reported. If so, one can see the status of the problem, when it was reported, and when a potential solution may be forthcoming.

Merchant solutions developer network: This page lists several dozen authorized Yahoo! developers who can help merchants take their stores to the next level. These developers are skilled at store redesigns, tool add-ons, conversion-enhancing features, and more.

Yahoo! badge program: Merchants who want to show their Yahoo! brand can add Yahoo!-approved badges (logos) to their site. This page includes three logos with detailed instructions on how to add the badges to their Yahoo! stores.

Yahoo! store blog: The Yahoo! store blog offers merchants tips and tricks for making their online stores successful. Past blogs are accessible on the right-hand side of the page and are sorted by category (e.g., Best Practices, Customer Service, Getting Started, Marketing/Promotion) and by date. This interactive page serves as a nice resource for merchants to learn from marketing experts and other small business owners. Links to other Yahoo! blogs and resources are also available as additional resources.

Yahoo! store help: This page offers a comprehensive list of resources for Yahoo! storeowners. It is sorted by category and allows merchants to access help for Getting Started (open for business checklist, general information, billing, about Yahoo! merchant solutions, managing your domain, and business mail); Building Tools (store editor, catalog manager, Web hosting, and store tags); Managing; Order Processing and Promoting (order settings, site settings, statistics, order processing, checkout manager, promoting, shipping, and risk tools); and Further Resources (guides and resources, troubleshooting, and release notes). While all of this information is available in other locations, Yahoo! makes it easy for merchants to find tools in multiple locations.

In addition to these menu categories and sub-categories, the Yahoo! Store Control Panel offers a search box to help merchants locate topics of interest, product tips, special Yahoo! marketing promotions, and the opportunity to join Yahoo!'s user research program.

While the Store Control Panel may seem overwhelming at first glance, it is well organized and relatively easy to navigate. Yahoo! includes plenty of help screens, FAQs, and descriptive text to help users find their way. Even those who are uncomfortable with technology should find the menus and help tools useful.

Web Hosting Control Panel

If you have a Web Hosting account instead of one for Merchant Solutions, you also get a number of different technical services. The Control Panel offers you a variety of tools to manage your Yahoo! Web accounts, including the following:

Home page: On the home page of this panel, users can access their business e-mail account(s), design tools, and promotional options. This page also contains a site activity summary for the last week and month. Merchants can see at a glance how many Web surfers have browsed their site.

E-mail: Merchants can add business e-mail addresses here.

Create and update: This page includes the following creation and updating features:

Basic site building tools: From this menu, users can design or redesign their Yahoo! stores using Site Solution, FrontPage, SiteBuilder, or additional Yahoo! tools.

File management tools: This menu gives users different options for uploading, organizing, and managing files using FTP settings, Easy Upload, or File Manager.

Blogging: For Yahoo! merchants who use blogs, this menu offers a blog manager, access to WordPress blogs, and basic and advanced blogging tools.

Other site building and editing tools: This section offers users more tools to enhance and customize their sites, including add-ons, custom error pages, HTML editor, MySQL database, Perl editor, PHP editor, PHP functions, PHP/Perl mail, and text editor.

Learning resources: The last category on this page directs users to other resources, including a Web hosting glossary (an alphabetical listing of Web and Web hosting-related terms), reference books (e.g., FrontPage, JavaScript, and Perl), and a handful of Yahoo! resource centers.

Each of these tools requires a certain amount of Web knowledge, but Yahoo! makes help available. For those who are Web savvy and who have the time and patience to personalize their Yahoo! stores, Yahoo! offers a good variety of Web creation and updating options.

Manage: The Manage tool contains the following three panels of options and is designed to give sellers a snapshot of regularly used management tools and site statistics:

Site management tools: From here, users can start or manage a blog, recover earlier versions of their Web site, use the secure server, and access file manager and password manager.

Site status: This panel allows users to view how much of their data storage space has been used, according to the type of merchant account they have. This area also includes links to service announcements for Yahoo! site updates and to upgrade your plan.

Web hosting account details: This section provides a snapshot of key details of your Web hosting account, including your domain name, FTP settings, and merchant plan details. It also includes a link to current Yahoo! promotions.

Promote: This page of the Web Hosting Control Panel offers multiple free and paid options for promoting your Web store, some of which are also available via the Store Control Panel. Because we will spend more time on marketing and promotion later, we will only include a brief summary here:

Free Yahoo! services: Yahoo! store merchants can see what search engine submissions Yahoo! has made on its behalf. Submission to Yahoo! and Google are included. Users can also sign up to get a free Yahoo! Local Listing.

Special offers: Here Yahoo! lists its current promotional offers:

Promote your site: Yahoo! offers users a list of tools for marketing and promoting their site online, some of which are accessible elsewhere. The tools include Yahoo! sponsored search, Yahoo! Search Submit Express, Yahoo! Local Sponsored Search, Google Adwords, and Submitnet.

Directory listings and ads: Merchants can use additional directory listings and ads to promote their Yahoo! stores. Options include Yahoo! Directory Submit, Yahoo! Local Enhanced Listing, and Yahoo! Sponsor Listings.

Online shopping distribution: Users can list their products at different sites, including Yahoo! Product Submit, Shopping.com, and Shopzilla, on a cost-per-click basis. **Shopzilla.com** is a shopping search engine that helps shoppers find the products they want to buy. Each of these pay-per-click services can be accessed using the Promote tab of the Web Hosting Control Panel.

Direct marketing and online ad tracking: From this section, Yahoo! Web hosting customers can access direct marketing and online ad tracking.

Help: The help page is broken down into two very useful sections: essential reading and Web hosting help home. The essential reading includes articles that are particularly beneficial for new Yahoo! merchants. Topics include getting started, control panel overview, and choosing a site-building tool. If you are not sure where to begin, this is the place. Next, Yahoo! offers four categories of Web hosting help with quick start, working with Web hosting, further learning, and Internet resources, all of which are good resources. If you cannot find what you need in the menus, Yahoo! offers customer service 24/7.

Index: Finally, the Web Hosting Control Panel includes a site-map-type index, which alphabetically lists topics and menu items, broken down into the following categories: home, e-mail, create and update, manage, promote, and help. This is simply another way of organizing the information that has already been presented.

Domain Control Panel

Whether you have just a Web Hosting account or have purchased a Yahoo! Merchant Solutions account, you will be given access to your Web site's domain control panel where you can manage the different aspects of your domain name (e.g., **www.yourbusi-**

nessname.com) and associated e-mail addresses (e.g., **you@your-businessname.com** and **info@yourbusinessname.com**). On this page, merchants can manage the following:

View/edit your domain name registration: Clicking on this link will show you how your domain name is registered, by whom, and at what address. The default option is for this information to be made public. For a small fee, however, Yahoo! will allow you to make this information private. If you want to protect yourself from spam, identity theft, fraud, and junk mail, this is an affordable option.

Manage your domain and sub-domains: Using this feature, domain customers can manage domain names and add sub-domains for Web sub-pages (e.g., info. page).

Manage advanced Domain Name Server (DNS) settings: Here, users can view and modify advanced domain name records. Yahoo! recommends that only advanced users use this option.

Domain name locking: Users can lock or unlock their domain names using this tool. By locking your domain name, unauthorized users cannot transfer your domain name or modify your name servers without your permission. Unless you are making changes to the name servers, it is recommended that users keep their domain names locked at all times.

E-mail: Yahoo! allows account holders to edit, add, and delete business e-mail accounts using this utility.

View your authorization code: If you need to transfer your domain name to a new provider, you will need this authorization code to make the transfer. This helps to prevent unauthorized transfers from one provider to another.

E-mail Control Panel

This tool offers another location for accessing your business e-mail accounts. From this control panel, you can check your business e-mail account(s); add e-mail aliases; add, edit, or remove e-mail addresses; and manage your business e-mail using a preferred POP3/SMTP e-mail account (e.g., Outlook, Outlook Express, or Thunderbird).

Summary

Using these four main control panels — Store Control Panel, Web Hosting Control Panel, Domain Control Panel, and E-mail Control Panel — Yahoo! store owners can access virtually all that Yahoo! has to offer pertaining to their merchant accounts. Merchants can not only access their individual information unique to their stores, they can also access customer service, help screens, and internal and external resources to help them set up, open, and manage their Yahoo! stores. Some menus and tools are more complicated to use than others, but most are designed to be user-friendly. Take some time to explore the possibilities Yahoo! has to offer.

CASE STUDY: KEVIN RICHARDS

Kevin Richards, CEO
Ventura Web Design
5803 W. Craig Rd. #108
Las Vegas, NV 89130
1-866-515-2057
www.venturawebdesign.com/

Starting a Yahoo! store takes a variety of skills. First, as with any business, a merchant needs to have business development and strategic abilities. Second, building a Yahoo! store takes entrepreneurial spirit. No business grows without plenty of hard work. Third, someone in e-commerce needs a basic understanding of the Internet and comfort with electronic media. In other words, it takes a special person to be successful.

No one has to do all this alone. Yahoo! provides support. In addition, there are a number of online businesses that deal directly with the Yahoo! store merchants and provide the support they need. Kevin Richards, CEO of Ventura Web Design in Las Vegas, offers this assistance. Richards came from a telecommunications background, even before the rise in popularity of the Internet. Before starting Ventura, he served as a software engineer for a local Bulletin Board System that allowed customers to log in via dial-up modem and play games, send e-mails, and chat on a closed network. "It is amazing how quickly things have changed in such a short time," says Richards.

He founded Ventura Web Design in 1997 with one goal in mind: To help small businesses make money through the Web.

CASE STUDY: KEVIN RICHARDS

"Today, with over 1,000 stores built and a decade of experience, we are one of the most successful Yahoo! store designers." Richards became involved with Yahoo! because "It's a great platform for anyone who's serious about e-commerce, but doesn't have $150,000 to develop and maintain a server and custom platform." Ventura has Yahoo! clients who have sold more than $30 million in a single year on this platform. "So, unless you are bigger than that, there is no reason to look elsewhere," he stresses.

Richards explains that excellent customer service, reliability, and dedication to customer success have made the company what it is today. "We are not the biggest team, which makes us able to focus on our clients instead of where we're going to get the next sale. We stay tuned in on what matters most to our clients." The organization works closely with clients "to push them to grow," says Richards, adding that they are "looking for entrepreneurs with a strong drive for success." One of the company's star clients is Organize.com, which sold more than $10 million in products last year. The store came to Ventura when the company was first started, and Ventura has "helped them at every stage of growth. Today, they are celebrating being listed as an Internet Retailer Top 500 Store."

Richards encourages potential clients to give serious thought to how they spend their time with their store. The best way to be productive is to do what they do best and then turn to others, such as Ventura, for other areas of expertise for improving and customizing their stores.

CASE STUDY: KEVIN RICHARDS

…Ventura has Yahoo! clients who have sold over $30 million in a single year on this platform.

CHAPTER 11

Running Your Yahoo! Store

You have created and published your Web store and are ready to promote it. In this chapter, we will offer detailed advice on your next steps, including how to launch your Yahoo! Web store and how to manage its daily operations. We will cover key topics for ensuring your store's success, including:

- Initial launch
- Simple promotional e-mail
- Press releases
- Maximizing sales
- Order processing
- Payment processing
- Shipping
- Taxes
- Bookkeeping
- Inventory management
- Site management
- Communication with customers
- Working with international customers

Initial launch of your Yahoo! Store

At this stage, we will assume that you have already published your store to the Web. It is live, you have reviewed it, and you have placed a test order that went smoothly. Now that you are comfortable that your site is ready to go, it is time to tell the world about your store. Initially, we will start with a few basic marketing and promotional tools, so you can test them out. This is sometimes called a "soft launch." Next, as your first orders come in, you can test and tweak your store. After that, you will be ready to seriously promote your store. At that point, you will be ready to move onto and cover marketing basics, as well as traditional and online marketing and promotional tools, to ensure the success of your first Yahoo! store. For now, we will start with two simple, affordable promotional tools.

Grand Opening E-mail to Family and Friends

In its infinite wisdom, Yahoo! has created a simple promotional e-mail tool that any merchant can use, regardless of computer savvy and marketing knowledge. It is aptly named "Simple Promotional E-mail" and can be accessed from the Store Control Panel. Here, Yahoo! has provided a grand opening e-mail template that is virtually ready to go. All you need to do is customize it by selecting the products to display, any special offers you want to make (e.g., percentage off or free shipping), and adding e-mail addresses. Within minutes, your free announcement is ready to preview and send. Yahoo! has made this step so simple that every merchant should be able to easily use this promotional tool.

If you already have an e-mail provider or list that you have not imported into Yahoo!, you can create your own welcome e-mail to send to family and friends. If you want to write it yourself, I recommend keeping the text simple and staying away from overly aggressive marketing language. Instead, try an upbeat but low-key approach. Here is an example:

"Greetings, family and friends. I am excited to tell you that I launched my first Yahoo! store today to share my love of antique trains and toys with people like you. I hope you will check it out and forward this link to anyone else you think might be interested. Thanks for your support."

Issuing a Press Release

Whether you are a marketing pro or a novice who just wants a successful business, issuing a press release is an easy, affordable way to spread the word about your new Yahoo! store. A press release is a fact-filled document of 300 to 500 words that tells local media and online media outlets about something newsworthy, such as a business launch, new product line, company anniversary, or industry award. It should be written with a professional, news-like tone rather than being filled with flowery adjectives boasting about how amazing your company is, and it should contain key information, including the news itself and where to go for more information. (In the Appendix, you will find a sample business launch press release and a press release template.)

Once your press release is written, be sure to proofread it carefully for errors. Ideally, have a second person read it who has an eye for detail, particularly if this is your first press release. Once you have your copy ready to go, develop a media list of where to send it. Gather e-mail addresses, mailing information, and fax numbers for local media and other interested organizations, including daily newspapers, community newspapers, radio and television stations, and your chamber of commerce or other networking groups to which you belong. Whenever possible, e-mail the press release to your intended recipients following these important guidelines:

- Send your press release in the body of an e-mail. Never send attachments unless requested to do so.

- Put your e-mail address (yourname@yourbusinessname. com) in the "To:" field and all other recipients in the "Bcc:" field. This will protect the privacy of the individuals to whom you are sending the press release. For example, newspaper A will not know that you also sent the press release to newspaper B and to the Center City Chamber of Commerce.

- List your complete contact information at the bottom of the press release. This information used to be at the beginning of the press release, but it is now preferred to submit this information last so the focus is on the news, not you.

- Conclude your press release with ###. To journalists, this denotes the end of the press release.

- If you have photos or logos available, indicate this at the bottom of the press release, but do not send those files without being asked for them.

- Be sure to include a relevant subject line, so recipients can decide whether they want to open the press release. We recommend a subject like this: NEWS RELEASE: Antique Train Enthusiast Launches Web site for Train Lovers. Note that we used the word NEWS instead of PRESS. To us, it is a press release. To the media, however, we want them to see our press releases as news.

- Do not badger the media for choosing not to "pick up" your press release. Sometimes they will, and sometimes they will not. It depends on many factors, including what other news is presenting itself on the day you distribute your press release. We have had the most success by distributing press releases on Tuesdays, Wednesdays, and Thursdays.

Press releases can also be distributed online to both free and paid distribution services. Popular paid services include PR Web, PR Newswire, and Marketwire. There are also many free services, such as Free Press Release and 1888 Press Release Network. By distributing online, you are creating an additional Web presence. For little or no money, you can quickly spread the word about your business and increase your search engine ranking. There is no guarantee that the local media will pick up your news item, but using online press release distribution channels is a good, inexpensive way to drive traffic to your site and get search engines to recognize your existence.

With these two marketing ideas, you have started the complex, fickle marketing and promotion process. These ideas are enough to get you started. We will cover other marketing and promotional tactics later. For now, we will move on to managing the day-to-day operations of your Yahoo! store.

Managing Your Store: Day-to-Day Operations

So you have launched your store, and orders are steadily coming in. Let us discuss how you will juggle all the activities of managing an online store.

Maximizing Sales

While many goals of business ownership will change, one will remain the same — you want to maximize sales every day. It is one thing having a Web site up and running, and a completely different thing obtaining and growing a customer base. In addition to maximizing sales by offering coupons, free shipping, gift certificates, up-selling, and cross-selling, you can also maximize your sales by offering sales, like 20 to 40 percent off either the entire sale or just one or two items.

Order Processing

You will want to set up a system for regularly processing customer orders. Consider how frequently you will do this — once a day, twice a day, or during business hours only. Also, determine who will be responsible for orders. Initially, you may be the sole person to receive, process, and fill orders. If so, make sure you have a back-up person, in the event that you are not available. Your back-up person will need to be trained and should be given an appropriate level of access to your merchant account.

To provide the best customer service, which will bring repeat business, it is important that your order processing routine is consistent. When you first get started, particularly if sales are slow, you may be in a position to process each one as it comes in. Once business picks up, however, you may not have this luxury, so choose a routine that is adaptable and efficient for both you and your customer.

Processing Online Orders by E-mail or Fax

For orders made online through your Yahoo! store, you can set your store options to send confirmations of new orders to you via e-mail, fax, or both. [*Note: the fax option is only available to merchants who purchase the Standard or Professional package.*] If others will also be processing orders, the confirmations can be sent to multiple people at different e-mail addresses.

For this example, we will assume an online order has been placed by a customer. Placement of the order by your customer includes production selection and purchase, as well as payment approval. While much of the work has been done, you will still want to review the order and continue processing it through to completion.

1) Begin by logging into your Yahoo! Small Business Merchant Account.

2) Go to Manage Your Services and select the "Store Control Panel."

3) From the Process column, select "Orders." You may be asked for your Security Key during this step, so be prepared to provide it.

4) Select the order you want to view using one of the search options and click the "View" button.

5) Review the order information. If the order looks all right, scroll down to the "Sale" button and click it. This will put

payment for the sale into queue so that it is batch-processed later that day.

6) Even though you have an initial approval code for a credit card sale, it could still be declined at this stage. Another window will appear showing you that the order was processed properly or that it failed. If it failed due to a declined payment method, you will need to contact the customer for an alternate form of payment.

7) Click the "OK" button. Repeat the process for additional pending orders.

Processing Phone Orders

Customers may shop at your Yahoo! store who are either unwilling or unable to process the order over the Internet. They may prefer to call you to place the order instead. At that point, you have two options to process the sale. You can place the order online yourself while you have the customer on the phone, or you can gather all the needed information from the customer and input it later into your order processing system. The latter option, however, carries with it greater risks, including violating security protocols. We highly recommend that you place the order online while the customer is still on the phone. This will be particularly helpful if the payment is declined for some reason. You will not have to call the customer back with questions or to get another method of payment. To process the order this way, follow the same steps as a customer ordering online.

1) From the product catalog, select the item(s) to be purchased

2) Click on "Add to Cart"

3) An order summary will appear. Select "Checkout" or "Checkout with PayPal"

4) Fill in the customer's shipping information (name, address, phone number, and shipping method) and click "Continue"

5) Choose the customer's preferred payment method from the choices offered (these choices will be based on how you originally set up your merchant account) and the e-mail addresses

6) If the customer has a coupon code, enter it in the box

7) Add any pertinent comments

8) On the payment screen, complete the customer's credit card information, including card number, expiration date, and the three-digit code on the back of the credit card

9) Process the payment according to the on-screen instructions, and provide the customer with the order number

Payment Processing

How and when you process payments will depend on the type of merchant account you have and what payment options you offer your customers. Some merchants will use their PayPal account, which allows customers to pay from their own PayPal accounts or with a major credit card, even if they do not have their own PayPal account.

Often, credit card payments are batch-processed once a day, depending on your merchant account provider. Even if you process each payment as it comes in, the payments will not actually go through your bank until the batch-processing is complete.

Retrieving Orders

The process for retrieving orders is the same as that listed in the order processing section.

1) Go to the Store Control Panel

2) From the Process menu, select "Orders" to go to the Order Manager

3) When new orders are pending, the Orders* link will include a red asterisk

4) From the Order Manager, you can view a single order or a range of orders, see a summary of orders, print orders, or export them to a database, such as Access, Paradox, or Excel

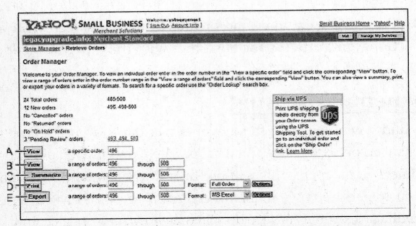

You can see in the screenshot that three orders are "Pending Review" orders. Then it gives their numbers — 493, 494, and 503. These are the order numbers of the files to be reviewed. You can also see where the owner wants to "View" order numbers 496-503. This will give the owner the opportunity to view and review the orders.

Canceling Orders

As you go through each new order in your Yahoo! Order Manager, you will have the ability to mark it as OK, fraudulent, canceled, returned, on hold, or pending review. If you have not processed a given order or clicked on the "Sale" button, you can still cancel the order. If you cancel an order, mark the transaction as "Canceled" in the "Mark Order" box and then hit the "Update/Modify" button. If you do not cancel the order using these steps, Yahoo! will charge you a transaction fee for that order. The percentage fee depends on the type of plan you purchased (1.5 percent for starter stores, 1 percent for standard, and 0.75 percent for professional). The order will be removed from your sales statistics.

Voiding Orders

If you have already processed an order and clicked on the "Sale" button, you can still void the order if it has not been batch-submitted. If you have processed the order and submitted the batch, you will have to issue a credit.

To void an order, go to the Store Manager and click on the "Orders" link. Retrieve the order to be voided. Scroll down until you see the "Void Sale" button, next to the Sale button. Click on the "Void Sale" button. The transaction will be removed from your sales statistics. If you get an error message that no transaction is pending, it means you have already processed the batch and will need to issue a credit instead.

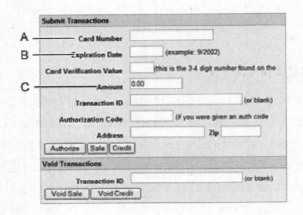

Figure 1: Manual Transactions page with required fields

Transaction	mystore-man-51864652332156 Sale 1.00
Card	1234567890123456 01/2004
Address Info	
Result	OK
Auth Code	026128
Details	Invoice = 40

OK

Figure 2: Confirmation page with status

In Figure 1, this is the transaction that you want to void; put that information in here.

In Figure 2, this is your confirmation page that confirms that the transaction is complete.

Crediting Orders

If you processed the order, and the batch has been submitted already, you cannot cancel or void the sale. You will have to issue a credit instead. You can also use this process for issuing a full or partial refund for a return. Go to the Store Manager and click on the "Orders" link. Retrieve the order to be credited. Scroll to the bottom of the order and type in the amount of the credit. The credit may be for the entire amount, in the event of a duplicate order, or a lesser amount, if you are only giving partial credit for a return (e.g., damaged or restocking fee). Then click on the "Credit" button.

Fraud Detection

Sadly, fraud detection is no longer just an occasional business activity. In this fast-paced, one-click-transaction world, there are many opportunities for fraud to occur, particularly in online business transactions. Unfortunately, if you are accepting phone and mail orders, your bank cannot protect you.

To protect yourself, here some warning signs of fraud. These are factors to consider when reviewing an incoming order. They are not guarantees that an order is fraudulent, but rather red flags to watch out for:

- **A suspicious shipping address.** According to Yahoo!, orders from certain countries have a high incidence of fraud and often have unverifiable addresses. Yahoo! cautions that you avoid orders from these countries unless you have considerable experience with international orders or can verify the orders in advance: Romania, Macedonia, Belarus, Pakistan, Russia, Lithuania, Egypt, Nigeria, Columbia, Malaysia, and Indonesia.

- **Untraceable e-mail address.** Fraudulent orders are often placed by people using free e-mail addresses from services like Yahoo!, Hotmail, and G-mail because these accounts are difficult to trace.

- **Expensive items.** Big orders, particularly for expensive or brand name items, may be a sign that an order is fraudulent. Any order with a larger total than normal should be investigated in more detail.

- **Multiple items.** It is unusual for one buyer to purchase multiple items like watches, televisions, or iPods or other mp3 players. These items have a high resale value and could indicate that the order is fraudulent.

- **Overnight shipping.** Yahoo! cautions that most fraudulent orders request overnight or express shipping, because the buyer is not worried about cost. In addition, the order may be shipped and received before it is determined to be fraudulent or the payment declined.

- **Shipping and billing address are different.** It can be risky to ship to one address while billing to another, unless it is clear that the purchase is a gift being sent directly to the recipient or that the buyer is having a purchase shipped to a work address, rather than a home address. Some merchants have made it a policy to only ship to the billing address. Setting such a policy, however, may create a problem for gifts orders.

- **Suspicious billing address.** Fraudulent orders may use a P. O. Box or a fictitious address (e.g., 123 Cherry Blossom Lane or Center City, Iowa 99999). To verify a legitimate address, you can use Yahoo! Maps, MapQuest, Microsoft Streets & Trips, or even the U.S. Postal Service's Web site.

- **Orders at new Yahoo! stores or Web sites.** Sometimes newly opened sites become targets for fraud, because the owners are assumed to be inexperienced in identifying potential fraud.

- **Drop-off orders.** If someone places a large order and asks that it be dropped off at the front door or another highly visible location, this could be a signal that the thief is going to pick up the package from that spot without signing for it.

- **Multiple orders from the same credit card.** If someone places multiple orders using the same credit card, this could be a sign that the orders are fraudulent.

- **Multiple credit cards from the same IP address.** If someone places orders with different credit cards, but from the same computer (and IP address), this is a red flag.

- **Credit card does not match the AVS verification.** If the billing address does not match the address on the credit card, the order could be fraudulent.

You do not have to tolerate fraud. Here are some methods you can employ immediately to help you detect and prevent fraud if you do not have the funds available for fraud protection software.

- Remember that obtaining an authorization number for a credit card charge does not guarantee that an order is not fraudulent. It only checks for two things: first, that the card has not been reported stolen, and second, that there is sufficient credit available for the purchase.

- Use an address verification service (AVS). It compares the customer's billing address with the address on file with the credit card issuer to ensure that it matches. This is a helpful safeguard, but it does not protect the holder of a stolen card from having purchases shipped to an alternate address. Also, AVS is only available for addresses in the United States. If you ship internationally or sell downloadable products, you have no protection.

- Verify unusual "Ship To" addresses, such as requests to send the package as a "gift" to a different address, most notably, a foreign address. Thieves frequently use this approach to send a product to a location where they can pick it up without being tracked. Normally, calling the cardholder will clear up any doubts.

- Look for big spenders, since thieves will frequently pay large fees to ship products quickly. They also like big-ticket purchases. If they can use the stolen card, receive the merchandise, and resell it quickly, they make a large profit. Detecting such activities and following up on them early can save you money in the long run.

- Ask for both a home and work phone and do a telephone number search on potentially fraudulent phone numbers. You can do this online by doing a reverse lookup on the phone number at sites like **www.anywho.com** or **www.reversephonedirectory.com**. Some of the services are free, but most charge a small fee for more information concerning a specific phone number.

- Put fraud notification messages on your Web site and order forms. This will not stop fraud, but thieves may think twice about using someone who puts such an emphasis on this problem.

- Make a list of any names, e-mails, or addresses that are questionable. If any new orders are similar to these in any way, check them out. Look for unusual quantities, duplications, and types of products.

An order meeting one or more of these criteria does not mean it is fraudulent. To protect yourself and provide the best customer service, you want to perform due diligence at this point. Telephone the customer and verify the information provided. Perhaps a simple error was made. This may include asking the customer to verify the name and address of the credit card issuer. If the customer has possession of the card, it should be easy to provide this information.

Additional Fraud Safeguard from Yahoo! — IP Blocking

After you have identified an order as fraudulent, you can block that person from ordering again using the same IP address. To block that address, go to the Store Control Panel in the Order Settings column, select "Risk Tools" and click on "IP Blocking." Type in the IP address you want to block, and click the "Add" button. You can block up to 100 IP addresses or ranges of addresses, but you can only add 10 at a time. You can also look to see who the ISP is and where the IP address originated. If you suspect fraud, you can contact the ISP for additional assistance or to warn it of potential fraudulent activity at that IP address.

Shipping

Again, shipping options will depend on how you set up your Yahoo! store initially. To review your options, go to the Yahoo! Shipping Manager. Ideally, you will consider using UPS Online Tools as a shipping partner, because it easily integrates with Yahoo!'s existing system. This makes it easier for the customer and for you.

It is a good idea to maintain contact with your customer throughout the ordering and shipping process. You can set up alerts to this automatically in Yahoo!:

1. Go to the Store Manager and click on the "Shipment and Order Status" link under Order Settings.

2. Under Shipment Tracking, make sure the Use Shipment Tracking Features box is checked.

3. For Order Confirmation E-mail, indicate the "from" address that will appear when the e-mail is sent to your customer, confirming the order (e.g., orders@yourstore.com or sales@yourstore.com).

4. Under Bounced E-mail Message, indicate a new e-mail address, or leave it blank to use the same address specified in step #3 above. This address is where "bounced" e-mail messages will go in the event that a customer gives you an invalid e-mail address.

5. In the Confirmation E-mail Box, type in your customer's confirmation message. If you do not type in a specific text, Yahoo! will provide a basic confirmation message. Click on "Preview E-mail" if you want to see how your message will look to the customer.

6. In the Status Update E-mail, type in your customer's status update message. If you do not type in a specific text, Yahoo! will provide a basic status update message. Click on "Preview E-mail" if you want to see how your message will look to the customer.

7. When you are done making changes to this screen, click "Update" to return to the Store Manager.

Packaging

Part of shipping, of course, involves packaging. Even if the products you sell are already packaged, you probably want to provide some additional packing materials (e.g., bubble wrap, cushioning, or Styrofoam peanuts) and some marketing materials in each box. The result should be a well-wrapped, secure — but economically efficient — package that will make it safely to its destination in one, attractive, well-labeled piece.

Bookkeeping

Yahoo! provides sales, revenue, and tax summaries to its merchants. This will suffice for basic bookkeeping purposes, but you should plan for a complete bookkeeping system separate from your Yahoo! account. Many small businesses use software programs like QuickBooks or Peachtree Accounting Software to track their income and expenses. Others employ a bookkeeper or an accountant to reconcile their books and to calculate and pay taxes. When first starting your business, it is a good idea to consult with a small business advisor or SCORE volunteer to get recommendations for bookkeeping systems and procedures. By starting out with solid financial practices, your bookkeeping — and income and expenses — will be much easier to track.

Taxes

Your tax needs will depend on the type of business you have. Service businesses typically do not have sales tax, but retail businesses will have different kinds of taxes, including sales tax.

Inventory Management

Handling your Yahoo! store's inventory will vary based on where your inventory is stored. If you keep it on site (e.g., in a warehouse next door or in your basement), your inventory will be readily accessible and trackable. When your inventory comes from an external source, such as a drop-shipper, you have little if any control over inventory, but overhead costs and storage problems are eliminated.

The most important points to know are what products you have in stock, how many units of each you have on hand, how many units you anticipate needing over the next 30 to 60 days, and how quickly you can re-order additional inventory from external sources. This information should be stored in a comprehensive inventory list, such as the Configure Inventory tool Yahoo! provides; a database that integrates with Yahoo!, like OrderMotion; or a free-form database designed to meet your specific needs.

For the purpose of this book, we will show you how to set up Inventory Management using Yahoo!.

1) Go to the Store Control Panel and select "Configure Inventory" from the Order Settings menu.

2) Choose from the three available inventory options: none, real-time inventory, and database inventory.

3) To set inventory levels, go back to the Store Control Panel and select "Inventory" from the Process menu.

4) Click "Edit" and update the quantity for each product. When finished updating the information, select "Save."

Restocking Inventory

Tip #1: Meet or exceed your customers' expectations every time. If you say you are going to ship an order within ten to fourteen days, meet or beat that period. If you fail to meet the customer's expectations, it is likely that the customer will not buy from you again. However, if you meet or exceed his or her expectations, you may have secured yourself a loyal customer.

In addition, there are federal regulations that apply, including the Federal Trade Commission's Mail or Telephone Order Rule. For more information about this rule and how it applies to your online business, visit the FTC online at www.ftc.gov.

Tip #2: Maintain contact. Even if you cannot meet a stated deadline due to uncontrollable circumstances, stay in touch with your customer to let him or her know about the delay and when the situation can be corrected. Leave messages or send e-mails to ensure that your customer is kept up to date on the situation and be prepared to make the situation right if the customer complains. Offer a discount on a future purchase, refund the cost of shipping, or send the customer a "thank you for your patience" gift. Rectifying the situation can go a long way toward repairing a potentially negative transaction.

Tip #3: Keep good records. To protect yourself from FTC claims or customer complaints, make sure you document each communication attempt with your customer. Document phone calls, voice mail messages, and save e-mails and notes of customer discussions or replies. If you save this information in chronological order, you can refer to it later to see what sequence of events took place and how you initiated or reacted to customer communication.

Tip #4: Each product should have a unique product code or number. This may be a number you create yourself, a SKU number, or a bar code.

Site Management

Web Site and Data Maintenance
Most users with basic Yahoo! store features will be able to man-

age their own Web sites using the tools and help provided. Others will want to contract with a Web designer or specialist to maintain their Web sites, making changes when needed. With a Yahoo! Web hosting account, however, many common Web site management tasks are included, such as regular backups and system updates.

Web Site Statistics

Whether you perform the above tasks yourself or hire a consultant or contractor to assist with them, you will want to monitor your Web site statistics personally on a regular basis weekly, or at least monthly. By tracking your Web stats, you can see what pages get the most hits, how many shoppers convert into buyers, and how many pages are being ignored or overlooked. By analyzing your Web traffic, you can also find out how people are finding your site. Did they find you from a search engine, the Yahoo! shopping directory, a pay-per-click ad, or some other source? This is key information that you will need to accurately monitor and measure your marketing plan. You need to know where your customers are coming from and how you can keep them coming back.

Communicating with Customers

Presumably, you are in business because you enjoy what it is that you do or sell. That passion should translate in your communications with customers. In other words, if you love what you do and believe in your products and services, communicating with customers should serve as an extension of that. When dealing with customers to verify orders, receive feedback, accept returns, or perform any other store-related function, keep these communication tips in mind:

1. The golden rule applies. Treat customers the way you want to be treated.

2. Each customer has the potential to offer referrals and repeat business. Ensure that the experience is a positive one to keep them coming back.

3. With the prevalence of social bookmarking these days (e.g., **Digg.com**, **del.icio.us**, **Technorati.com**, **StumbleUpon.com**, **reddit.com**, **BlinkList.com**, and **Furl.net**), every interaction has the possibility of spreading across the Internet in a matter of minutes. What will customers say about your store?

4. Until it is clear that a transaction is fraudulent, give the customer the benefit of the doubt.

Working with International Customers

As we discussed in the fraud detection section of this chapter, filling international orders can be dangerous with fraud being so rampant on the Internet these days. According to Yahoo! in its "Warning Signs of Fraud" help pages, fraud is less of a problem from customers ordering from North America, Western Europe, or Japan. Filling orders for buyers in these regions, however, is not a guarantee that the orders will be legitimate.

In addition to dealing with potentially fraudulent orders, if you decide to sell your products internationally, you will need to consider these questions as you set up your payment, shipping, and tax options:

•   Will you need to convert pricing to foreign currency?

- Will tax rates apply in regions outside your home country?

- What shipping options are available to you?

- Do any international or foreign government regulations (e.g., customs) apply?

You will need to set up such options in Shipping Manager, and you will need to know how to package and ship the items to international destinations.

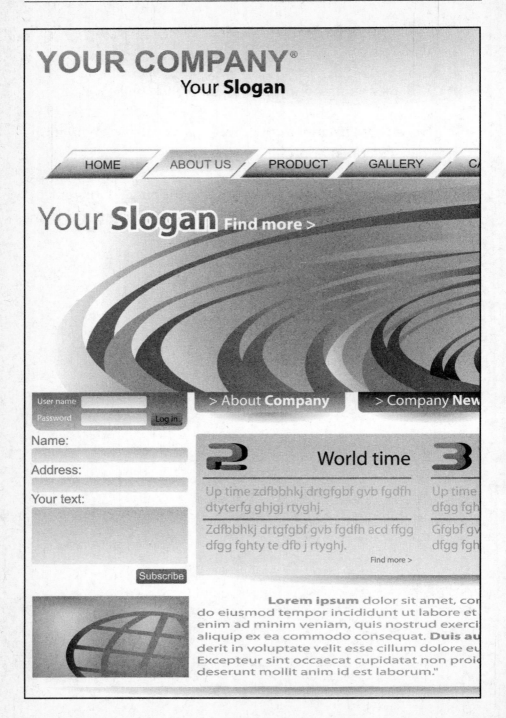

CHAPTER 12

Marketing Your Yahoo! Store, Part 1

Now that your store has been published to the Web, you will need to market and promote it to let people know it exists. In the last chapter, we gave you some initial marketing ideas to tell potential shoppers about your site, but there is much more work to be done to drive traffic to your store. First, we will discuss all the marketing possibilities. Then we will help you narrow down the tools and techniques that you will choose for your particular store and budget.

Opening your store actually requires little time and energy compared to what has to be done once your store is open and you want to make sure that people know that you exist, where you exist, and why you exist (to serve their needs, of course). It is not surprising that many store owners say that they spend a good ten to twelve hours a day working on their store to make it successful. There are many others who work part-time at their business, but their income is commensurate with their time commitment.

Recognizing Your Value

Whether you developed your business plan over months or years or created it in just a few days, opening your Yahoo! store is a big accomplishment. Ideally, it is something that you are passionate about and that you want to see succeed. What part of your store or your business makes you most proud? Do you have a unique business that no one else can duplicate? Maybe you offer an unusual product mix or the best prices. Perhaps your engineering background makes your handcrafted toy airplanes the best on the market. Those are the items that you will want to emphasize when marketing; but first, you have to recognize their value and then sell that value to your customers. We will start by listing your assets, or in marketing speak, your *unique selling proposition.*

Basic Marketing Principles

When many of us start out in the business world, we have a limited view of marketing. We believe that marketing consists of just two things: sales and advertising. While those are certainly important components of the marketing equation, they are by no means all-inclusive. No matter what your level of marketing experience, every online merchant needs to know a bit about marketing and promotions. We will cover some basic principles of marketing to give you a working knowledge from which to begin. Then we will give you specific ideas and tools for promoting your Yahoo! store, followed by a quick, easy method for marketing planning in your first year.

Consistent Contact

Marketing statistics show that it takes a business six to eight times of being seen or noticed by a potential customer before the customer will remember the name. That means that you need to be clear about who your target market is, and you need to reach it regularly. One e-mail blast and a one-time ad in your local paper are not going to be sufficient. You need to go where your customers are and reach out to them on a consistent basis.

Putting Yourself in Your Customer's Shoes

One of the easiest ways to figure out how to best reach your target customer is to put yourself in his or her shoes. To illustrate, we will assume that you have an online store of vintage books for sale. If you were looking for a particular edition of *Little Women*, for example, how would you look for a bookstore? Would you look in your local yellow pages, read the classifieds, search online, or go to a flea market? Think like your customer. Where would he or she go?

Promote Your Store Using Yahoo! Services

Yahoo! Promotional Tools

One of the keys to Yahoo!'s success is its ability to provide the average users with tools and techniques to promote their products and stores. Yahoo! has taken complicated concepts and broken them down into easy-to-follow and easy-to-understand instructions so that anyone who wants to own a successful Yahoo! store can do so. In this chapter, we will discuss some of those tools and how you can leverage them to drive traffic to your site, convert shoppers into buyers, and increase referrals and revenue.

- **Search engine marketing:** Search engine marketing consists of submitting your site to search engines and developing your site using search-engine-friendly content.

- **Keyword marketing:** This is the same as using tags on

some of your products, so when the keywords are put in the search engines, the product is found quickly, without the hassle of searching through unwanted products.

Yahoo! Sponsored Search

Have you ever searched online for a company or keyword and seen a highlighted box at the top of the page with two or three businesses listed? These are the types of ads available through Yahoo! Sponsored Search.

When you start your business, it will take time before the search engines begin to pick you up and visitors see your listing. Depending on how much copy the search engines have found on your Web site, this could take several months. In the meantime, you will want to do other things to let people know about your site and the product you have for sale. Sponsored ads are pay-per-click (PPC) ads that appear when people search using keywords. PPC has some tremendous advantages for online businesses.

Here is how it works: Merchants bid on keywords related to their products — for example, antiques, antique toys, antique trains, and antique toy trains. When a potential customer types those keywords into the Yahoo! search engine, your ad may appear in the search results. When and how often your ad appears depends on how many competitors have also bid on those keywords. You only pay your bid price each time your ad is clicked, not each time it appears. Starting at 10 cents per click, this is a good way to get your products in front of your targeted audience. Advantages include the following:

- You do not have to wait until the search engines pick up

your site. You can immediately drive traffic to your site.

- You only pay when someone clicks on your ad, regardless of the number of times your ad is shown. By carefully keeping track of your results, you can determine how well each ad is converting and whether you want to make changes or stop the ads.

- Because you are just starting out, you have a steep learning curve. With PPC, you can run several ads at the same time and readily see the ones that work best. Test your keywords this way, and use the best ones on your Web site to boost your search results.

Yahoo! Content Match

This Yahoo! product complements the Yahoo! Sponsored Search feature by displaying your ads next to related content, including articles and product reviews, on sites like Yahoo! and Viacom. Using this product gives you an additional source of targeted leads. Your bid price and tracking is separate from the Sponsored Search program, so you can track where your leads are coming from. Content Match can be done one of two ways. You can use exact keyword matches with minor variations, or you can use Yahoo!'s advanced match type, where you use keywords in different contexts. The advanced match option broadens your search results.

Yahoo! recommends using the content match tool for specific terms, rather than vague ones (plasma television versus television), to help you avoid unqualified traffic. Also, identify keywords that potential customers may use for your products; their keywords may differ from your own set of keywords. And choose keywords for each ad group carefully. You will want to choose the most appropriate keywords using the advanced option to bring in more potential customers.

Yahoo! Search Submit Express

This Yahoo! tool gathers relevant content from all over the Web to include in its Yahoo! Search Technology index. You can submit up to five URLs per domain name to be included in non-sponsored search results on Yahoo!, AltaVista, and AllTheWeb. Once your site's pages have been reviewed, relevant content will be included in targeted search results, driving traffic to your site. Web pages are usually reviewed within four days of submission. Following the initial approval, pages are refreshed every seven days. This tool allows you to track performance, so you can view which of your URLs are being clicked on and what their average ranks are in Yahoo!'s search results. In addition, this tool can analyze the meta tags for your submitted URLs and suggest ways of optimizing your pages.

Yahoo! Travel Submit

Merchants can promote their travel offers and deals through cost-per-click pricing with Yahoo!'s Travel Submit. Detailed listings of your travel offers and deals will be featured in highly relevant areas of Yahoo!'s Travel section — including Yahoo! Travel Deals and Yahoo! Travel Guides — putting you in front of a targeted audience of motivated travelers. You can manage your account online to update information quickly and to monitor the performance of your ads.

Google AdWords

This popular online tool works much like Yahoo!'s sponsored search tool. You create an ad that is displayed when a Web user types in certain keywords. Rotated with other merchants who have purchased the same keywords, your targeted ad will occasionally appear next to search results matching those keywords. You pay each time your ad is clicked on, not each time it appears. What is different about Google AdWords is that you do not need a Web site or Web page to participate. Google will help you create one for free. In this case, you have a Yahoo! Web store, so you can skip that step.

Additional Google Tools

Like Yahoo!, Google offers a full range of targeted ad opportunities. In addition to AdWords, merchants can target local and regional customers, get added to Google Maps, and post ads throughout Google's content network. For more details and pricing, visit **http://adwords.google.com**.

Submitnet

As one of Yahoo!'s business partners, Submitnet uses its online suite of seven site analysis, optimization, and tracking tools to help Web site owners, including Yahoo! merchants, to optimize their sites for search engines. In addition to offering reporting and tracking tools and unlimited e-mail support, Submitnet offers custom monthly submissions of your Web site to the most popular search engines.

In addition to these sponsored search and pay-per-performance tools, Yahoo! offers opportunities to its merchants for directory listings and ads. Here, we will discuss Yahoo!-specific tools, as well as other online tools that accomplish similar tasks:

Yahoo! Directory Submit

This tool is a site suggestion service where commercial business owners pay a fee (currently $299 per year) for an expedited review of their Web site by a member of Yahoo!'s editorial staff. Payment of the fee guarantees that Yahoo! will review your site and respond to you about its decision to include your site in the Yahoo! Directory within seven days. The fee is nonrefundable and is renewable per year. Payment of the fee is not a guarantee that Yahoo! will include your business in its directory, just that it will review your site within seven days. Additional restrictions apply, so contact Yahoo! for the latest details.

Yahoo! Product Submit

Yahoo! offers a product submission tool to help merchants promote their products in Yahoo! Shopping and other relevant Yahoo! sites, including Yahoo! Movies, Yahoo! Games, and Yahoo! Music. It matches detailed product descriptions from your Yahoo! store to consumer searches in Yahoo! Shopping on its product search and comparison product pages. This is a pay-per-click service where you pay each time someone clicks on your ad, rather than each time it appears. Some restrictions apply, so contact Yahoo! directly for details. Yahoo! store merchants receive a discount on the pay-per-click price.

Yahoo! Local Listings

As will be seen later on in the book, merchants can have different local listings in order to draw buyers who search with Yahoo! for top-rated places near them.

Local Basic Listings

For free, you can have a listing with the name and type of your business, location, telephone, fax, URL, e-mail, hours, payment choices, and products and services offered.

Local Enhanced Listings

If you pay a monthly charge of $9.95, you can add a logo, tagline, as many as ten visuals, and specific business overview to your Local Basic Listing. You can also be included in five business categories and have two links that can be customized for coupons or special offers.

Local Featured Listings

For $25 or more per month, the Local Enhanced Listing can be supplemented with highly visible placement in Yahoo! Local, monthly flat rate billing dependent on your store category and geographical area, an easily tailored listing and company details page, and a no-cost, basic Web site with up to five pages.

CHAPTER 13

Marketing Your Yahoo! Store, Part 2

Search Engine Optimization Highlights Yahoo! Stores

As the Web has become more sophisticated, so, too, has Web site marketing. With millions of Web sites competing for millions of potential buyers, it has become increasingly complex to find ways of ensuring that anyone who is interested in the products or services you offer can find your store. One of the most important ways to ensure that this is done is by having your Web site be visibly listed when someone puts your product or service into a search engine.

Yahoo! helps you get customers to your Web site with its strong branding and high ranking, but you need more. You have to make sure that your customers see your store when they put keywords into the search engines. At this point, we want to make sure that you understand the terminology.

- **Search Engine:** A Web-based service that looks across the entire Web for your search requests.

- **Directories:** "Search indexes" that, when people search inside them, direct people only to the site that is within the index. Directories are made up of businesses that have paid a fee to have their businesses listed. For example, if you want to have your store or business listed with the Yahoo! directory, which you do, you just pay the fee, which varies by the search engine for your listing. Then your registered business goes into a "categorized index" with other businesses with similar services or products. When a customer searches a directory using a keyword, the Web sites listed will only be those businesses in the directory, not the entire Web, as with Google. When you list your store or business with both the search engines and the directories, you get twice as much exposure to the entire world population through the Internet.

- **Search Engine Optimization:** The art (and it is an art) of getting your Web site found by search engines is called *Search Engine Optimization* (SEO). The people who specialize in this for a career are called "SEO experts" or "SEO companies." SEO has long been one of the most important subjects in online marketing. All Internet professionals have their own ideas on how best to get high rankings. Entire books have even been written about SEO. It comes down to this octopus-like creature, spreading itself across the Internet and looking for food to bring back to eat. In this case, it eats words and phrases, and it prefers the newest, most interesting food it can find. These octopi, or search engines, go out and hunt, retrieve, and collect information based on the keywords users request to have the most relevant results.

Search engine octopi, therefore, study the context of your Web pages and rank your content by hunting for specific phrases. They use two or more related words or phrases to garner the basic meaning of your page. Thus, in all your Web communication you need to provide the relevant copy with the words and phrases that will most attract these octopi. With our fictitious train site, we needed to use the phrase "antique locomotives" a reasonable number of times, so the search engines knew that the pages were generally about trains and, more specifically, antique trains. If the word is also placed in the title, then the search engines recognize that the article, and perhaps the whole site, is about this topic. If it grabs enough information from your pages that indicates that the site is about antique locomotives, it will rank the site for not only trains, but also similar terms.

The closer you are to the top of the first page, the more chance that visitors will click on your link and go to your site. If you do not have a high search engine ranking and end up 100 or more sites away from the first listings, only the ardent searchers will find you. Therefore, you want to maximize, or "optimize," your rankings in the search engines. In order to do this, you need to make sure 1) the search engines are interested in your Web site and pick up the information and 2) you use the same words and phrases in your copy that the people searching for your site type in.

To make matters more complicated, Google and the other search engines are continually changing their searching parameters. This is the reason for using qualified SEO experts who keep up with the latest changes, making sure that Web sites are search engine friendly (meaning that the search engines readily read them) and ensuring that you regularly use updated copy on your Web site and/or blog (since the search engines do not like old, stale copy).

Yahoo! starts you off on this process by automatically submitting your store to the major search engines when you first publish.

Bottom line: There are key phrases — research indicates that longer words grouped together do better than shorter ones — to use on your Web pages to attract the search engines, and thus, those who search with them. You can also find out, for example, through Google, what phrases are searched most and, even through Google's Trends, how popular certain search terms are across geographic regions, cities, and languages.

Do Not Go Overboard with SEO Keywords

Web site owners have learned, and often the hard way, that they cannot overload Web or catalog copy with keywords. You will be punished by being ignored for a long time. This approach does not work; the copy is almost unintelligible, and your customers will know what you are doing, just like the search engines do. The recommended keyword density ranges from 3 to 7 percent. Anything above this, even 10 percent density, starts looking like keyword stuffing. It is even more important to have the correct density in the title, headings, and first paragraphs. Use a word-density tool to determine whether your keywords are in the correct range. If not, find synonyms or rewrite the copy. At the same time, make sure that you do not have too many words in italic or bold face; these will also attract the search engines if not in the correct quantity.

Hidden texts are another trick that you cannot use. This is when the text and links are made the same color as the background. Search engines will not only pass these over, but may penalize you for such practices. Very similar to hidden links are doorway pages, which are written for high ranking in the search engines and not for human reading. Duplicate pages, with the same copy used repeatedly, are similarly nixed. These are also no longer acceptable. The search engines are just as stringent on the number of links per page, with both outbound and inbound links. There are also programs that can let you know whether your link density is acceptable.

Another SEO turnoff is using small or unreadable type to fit more words into the design of the Web Site. The biggest "do not" in terms of keywords is one that not only disturbs the search engines, but also the visitors. Do not put keywords into your copy that have nothing to do with the theme of the page. Today, keywords are important, but it is how they are used that matters.

Make sure your keywords appear in crucial locations, such as the title tag, which should have the most relevant three top keywords that visitors will use to search for your site. Use your keywords often, and make sure they appear high on your page. Make sure your Web pages hold the content of your keywords. If your site is on collecting antique trains, make sure your Web page talks about collecting antique trains and/or similar topics. Also, use your keywords in the meta-tags. Use meta-tag keywords and descriptions for your Web pages. As noted earlier, your product categories, subcategories, and descriptions should also have your keywords.

Some Additional SEO Tips

There are some basic things you can do to increase the chances that the search engines will pick up your copy. These include the following:

- Commit yourself to SEO. It is something that you need to work on at least once a day. The more you are committed to the process, the better the results will be.

- SEO should be part of your overall marketing plan. You need clear SEO goals and an outline of how you expect to achieve them, and at what cost.

- Be patient. After your Web site goes up, it will take at least two to three months of your hard editorial work to get the rankings you want in the search engines. The smaller and newer your business, the more difficult it becomes. That is why you want to continually work on this.

- Put at least a couple of topics of interest on your Web site every week using your keywords, which are original and not copied from someplace else. The search engines like new material. This also gives you an opportunity to write about any other information regarding your products.

- Build your Web site with a number of different pages and more copy. This gives you additional opportunities with the search engines. On each page you have online, there is another way to use keywords that will be searched and will reach specific potential customers. You can end up with hundreds of content pages, each one able to be indexed by the search engines. Usually the keywords that you find are most searched in your copy.

- Keep quality in mind at all times. You want strong editorial content that will be of interest to your readers and the search engines.

- Construct an interesting Web site, and always strive to make it better. That means adding content of interest to your main buyers.

- Do not forget your site map. Those octopi cannot index pages that cannot be crawled. Your site map will help the search engines understand the layout of your pages.

- When you decide on your URL, think SEO. Keywords in your Web site name are useful.

- Use all your keyword resources. We mentioned some of those above, such as Yahoo!'s help and Google's Ad-Words.

- Use a different, pertinent title and meta-description on each page. Remember that the title of the page is the most important SEO factor. The meta-description tag will not help in your ranking, but will appear in your listing and encourage people interested in the topic to look for more.

- Make your copy interesting for your primary readers. They are the ones who will be coming to your site and buying your products and services.

- You want copy that is different than other Web sites. This is difficult for people in e-commerce. Put some time into your descriptions of products, and stay away from the boilerplates from the manufacturers. If you put your keywords into your descriptions, you will be ahead of the pack.

- Use keywords as anchor text when linking internally.

These tell the search engines what the page is about.

- Send out press releases, but make them count. As we noted before, you want to send out a press release announcing your arrival into the virtual world. You should be considering sending out others, as well, because they can establish you as a good media source for your industry. Just make sure that your release is meaty and covers a topic of importance. Then it will be picked up by the media and blogs, as well as the search engines.

- Start a blog and participate with other related blogs. We cover this more in depth later. Just remember how important it is for SEO purposes.

- Social marketing is becoming an increasingly useful tool. Join the appropriate communities on Flickr and post visuals about your product. If you are a service-oriented business, use Yahoo! Answers to position yourself as an expert in your industry. Remember that this needs to be a two-way street. You are not using these vehicles just for your own purposes. You should become a contributor and support others who need reliable information. The same is true about forums. This will be covered later, as well.

Yahoo! Sponsor Listing and Shopping

As noted previously, a good way to spread the word about your store and its products and services is by sharing that information with online shopping distribution networks. By listing your products at different sites on a cost-per-click basis, you can control how often your name appears online, as well as how much you spend in PPC advertising. Yahoo! offers several tools for this type of advertising:

- **Shopping.com** – According to Yahoo!, **Shopping.com** is the Internet's fourth largest shopping site. It allows shoppers to compare and purchase all kinds of products.

- **Shopzilla** – **Shopzilla.com** is a shopping search engine that helps shoppers find the products they want to buy. After creating a Shopzilla merchant account and funding it with a refundable deposit of $50, merchants sign up to receive cost-per-click leads for their product listings. Product listings will appear across all Shopzilla sites, including BizRate and AOL's **InStore.com**. Shopzilla also offers business services with useful tools to manage your search engine promotions: bidding, listing management, and reporting tools.

Store Gift Certificates

If you use the Standard or Professional Merchant Solutions package, you can create and manage gift certificates in your Yahoo! store. You can create gift certificates from the Store Manager menu using the Store Editor or the Catalog Manager tools. You can create gift certificates at varying price points. You can advertise this service on your Web site, as well as in any of your e-mail marketing campaigns. This option will be particularly popular during the holidays and at other gift-giving times (e.g., birthdays, anniversaries, graduation, and weddings). *Note: To avoid issuing gift certificates to a fraudulent purchaser, wait until the order is fully processed before e-mailing or mailing the gift certificate.*

Yahoo! Groups and Other Online Forums

If you belong to a relevant Yahoo! Group or another related on-line forum, post a message inviting visitors to your site. Encourage them to share the link with others if they like your store, and ask for their feedback about what they like and do not like about your Yahoo! Web site. This information can be invaluable as you adjust your store's appearance, inventory, and order processing systems.

Yahoo! hosts groups for categories like animals, business and finance, computers and Internet, culture and community, entertainment and arts, family and home, games, governments and politics, health and wellness, hobbies and crafts, music, regional, religion and beliefs, romance and relationships, schools and education, science, and sports and recreation. Each category has a home page that lists its pick of the week and forums in various subcategories. The home page also contains links to the best forums in each category. For entrepreneurs, consider these groups: Small Business, Home Business, Moms United in Business, and Entrepreneurs at Home. Check out the groups that interest you, scroll through their most recent postings, and if you think you could contribute to the group and it could benefit you as well, click on the "Join This Group" link and follow the on screen instructions.

Thousands of other sites also offer online forums in which you can interact with like-minded individuals. Some that host groups include Google (**http://groups.google.com**), MSN (**http://groups.msn.com**), MySpace (**http://www.myspace.com**), Friendster, and more. There are also business-oriented online networking groups, like Linked In (**www.linkedin.com**), Konnects (**www.**

konnects.com), and BizWiz™ (**http://www.bizwiz.com**).

Providing a Positive Buying Experience

When you get your Yahoo! site up and running, you have to make sure that it gets the attention it requires, keeping visitors on the site longer and having visitors return on a regular basis. Through your Yahoo! participation, you will receive the foundation for attention-getting and promotion for your products. You need to build on that foundation to obtain optimal exposure for your merchandise. The Internet is huge, and without spending time on marketing and promotion, a small e-commerce store entity can quickly disappear.

Naturally, you want to have new visitors come to your Web site to buy your merchandise. Yet, it is equally important to provide a positive buying experience, so they will want to purchase from you again. You want your customers and potential buyers to appreciate coming to your Web site for other reasons than just looking at products. The longer they remain on your site, the better the chance for present and future sales.

It is also crucial to continually ask for feedback. One vendor, for example, has a note on the bottom of each of its Web site pages that says, "How are we doing with our Web site?" It is a good way to get advice from customers on how products can be displayed better or what is missing that customers want to see.

Yahoo's! Customer Rating System Lets Shoppers Vote

Shoppers always want to see how other buyers feel about products and services they plan on purchasing. Yahoo!'s Customer Rating system gives stores with the highest customer ratings the opportunity to brag to the world with special symbols next to their names in Yahoo! Shopping and on their Web sites. These ratings show old and new customers alike that they have been voted the best. It works like this:

- Merchants log into the Manager and turn on "Enable Ratings" in the Customer Ratings section for all products sold. Then they click on the "Publish Order Settings" link to make the change live.

- Buyers can find a box on their order for where they can rate the merchants on all orders.

- If shoppers opt to vote, they will receive an e-mail a few weeks later asking them about their experiences with the merchant based on a five-point scale.

- Based on the customers' responses, the store owners receive a certain number of stars. The more stars they get, the higher their rating. Merchants with the highest ratings will usually be higher in the Yahoo! Shopping search results, too.

- If merchants do not allow customer ratings, they cannot appear in Yahoo! Shopping.

- There are no negative ratings next to a business' name, only positive ones. Only buyers can change their rating. When doing so, only the most recent rating counts.

Stores can see their ratings when logging into the Manager on a bar graph.

Also, when a customer fills out the rating form, store owners get an e-mail message with the order identification number, rating, and comments. At times, customers decide to send their rating without an ID or to only show their rating with Yahoo! Shopping.

Here is an example of how a Yahoo! store owner uses the positive rating on the Web site as a marketing tool.

> **HTmarket.com** participates in the Yahoo! Shopping and Shopping.com ratings. In Yahoo! Shopping, we are rated 4.5 stars out of 5 rating scale and in **shopping.com**, we are rated 4.5 out of 5 check marks. These are very high ratings based on hundreds of customer ratings. We also carry the trusted store seal from **shopping.com**, which is awarded to their very top stores. **HTmarket.com** has been on the Web as retailer for five years. **HTmarket.com** has the best selection and the most products of any internet store for home theater. (See case study for HTmarket)

There are a number of concerns that customers have about their products. If you keep on top of such issues, your chances for getting a higher rating will be much improved.

- Update inventory daily. Customers are not pleased when they try to buy an item and it is out of stock. Similarly, check pricing regularly. When pricing your items, research competitive products and make necessary adjustments. If an item has not sold for over a month, check your price to make sure that it remains competitive.

- Although the customer will get an automated e-mail, you can send your own when you ship an item. Let the customer know it is on the way and by what method it is being shipped.

- Respond to refunds and returns in a timely manner.

- Answer all buyer inquiries within 24 hours of receipt. Good communication with customers promotes good feedback for sellers.

Here are some of the typical transaction problems:

- The item does not arrive, yet the customer is billed

- The product is sent with flimsy or inadequate packaging and labeling

- The item is received later than expected

- The order is canceled without notice, because it is out of stock or no longer available, although not listed as such

- The customer has difficulty returning an item and getting a refund

- The buyer cannot reach the seller through e-mail and no phone number is listed

- The condition of the item is not as described

- The model number or brand is different than the one ordered

- The item was not discounted as expected

CASE STUDY: ALAN HUTCHINSON

Alan Hutchinson, CEO
MarketWare Technologies, Inc.
5100 N. Ravenswood Avenue
Suite 100
Chicago, IL 60640
1-888-764-9273
www.htmarket.com

In eight years, he has expanded HT Marketplace to more than $5 million in sales.

Often, merchants will start a Web site when they see a specific need that is not being met. That is the case with Alan Hutchinson, CEO of Home Theater Marketplace. After the Internet started becoming popular, he began building Web sites for other companies and increased his competency on the ins and outs of this new electronic vehicle. In 1998, he was putting together a home theater and had to go to ten different vendors to find all the parts. "I thought at the time it would have been much easier to have one store online to get everything needed," he said, and thus, Home Theater Marketplace was born.

Hutchinson decided to use Yahoo! for his Web site, since "this was the biggest and best game in town at that time. They had some good things going, where merchants were automatically included in the shopping portal for the monthly fee. There was not pay-per-click then," he recalls. He designed the site by himself, and four years later, updated it with the help of a full-time Web master.

CASE STUDY: ALAN HUTCHINSON

Since then, Hutchinson's success has been phenomenal. In eight years, he has expanded HT Marketplace to more than $5 million in sales. He was fortunate to get involved during the first years. "The game has changed now since 2000, and you really have to have a sharp plan to get going. You just can't put up a site and expect it to begin selling as quickly as we did in 2000."

Hutchinson says that Yahoo! offers a solid back end, good uptime, and reliability. There are also many outside companies that work with owners to help them put up Yahoo! stores, as well as a support network. "The Yahoo! platform is still very much the same as it was in 2000, with some added features, but it is a stable cart. That's why we stay with it. I would suggest Web sites work with one of the outside consultants who handle Yahoo! design, since they know how to customize the store to your liking. The 'out-of-the-box store' does not do everything needed to compete, and the outside firms know how to get your site to the next level."

Hutchinson also recommends that new online merchants "must have a solid business plan before jumping into this. There is established competition with entrenched positions in many markets, including niche markets like ours. Make sure you have a plan and are totally committed to the site."

Using E-mails to Foster Relationships

From the very beginning of your online experience, you will want to start growing a list of names of customers and potential customers. As you build this list, think of the ways you can use it to grow your business, for example, through e-mail newsletters, e-mail store coupons, and free offerings. Always ask anyone who comes to your site to "opt" in. That means that this person, upon sending in his or her name and e-mail, is agreeing to receive e-mails from you. Promise that you will never give the name of your customers to other listings.

Because you do not actually see your clients, it is essential to build a relationship with them in other e-commerce ways. One of the most beneficial vehicles is e-mail, which can be used to respond to product questions, clear up misunderstandings, prevent any concerns that may come up in the future, and encourage higher rankings with customers. E-mail can also be used as a marketing vehicle to give the customers information on the latest products and the industry. As a seller, the customers' e-mails can offer insights on trends and let you see how you can best improve your customer service. Negative comments can be quite helpful. It is better to read such comments than have the customer never let you know and spread the word about the problems to others.

When you receive an e-mail with a question about one of your products for sale, it is important to respond within 24 hours. Think seriously about having a separate e-mail just for queries, since they may get lost with all the other mail you get during the day. You can get another e-mail account from Yahoo! so these comments are separated.

Take several minutes at the beginning of your day to check this feedback account and respond to customers. Even if you do not have any answers at that moment, or need additional information from the customer that is not explained in the e-mail, respond to the question. It is much better to send an e-mail with, "I will get back to you within 48 hours," or "Could you please give me more information regarding your concern," than responding late or not at all. To speed up the process with responses to such queries, you can copy and paste in a general response. This is recommended over sending out form letters. Customers want to be treated like "real people" and communicate with "real people," not automated responders.

After a sale is made, e-mails are just as important. With Yahoo! you can make e-mails go out automatically when the sale is complete and provide information on how and when items will be shipped. This is the perfect time to also write your own personal e-mail to the customer saying "thank you" for placing the order for (name of item) and asking to be contacted in case of any problem with the order once received, or if there is a delay for any reason. You are building a rapport with the customer while taking a preventative stance. A few weeks after the customer receives the product, send another e-mail asking whether everything is acceptable. If there were any problems, you want to know about them. This shows that you truly stand behind your service. If they are giving you a rating, this will be a plus. If they decided not to use the rating system and give you feedback, see whether you can use their comments for a testimonial.

You can also ask the customer to "opt in" for receiving a newsletter you publish every month or notice of sales events. (You will include a link where the customers can add their e-mail address and approve these monthly e-mails). You can also offer the customer a discount as a thank you for the present order. There may be an item you have on sale at the present time that you can use. Give the customer a special code to use when buying the item.

Of course, you never want to overdo it with e-mails, as with any other marketing vehicle. Yet, businesses have found that e-mail marketing works quite well:

- The Direct Marketing Association reports that e-mail marketing generated a return on investment (ROI) of $45.06 for 2008.

- **Shop.org** reports that e-mail-to-house files are one of the least expensive tactics in terms of cost per order, or $6.85 at an average dollar value of $120.27 per order.

- According to MarketingSherpa, the recession is putting increased emphasis on ROI in marketing campaigns, and e-mail stands out as a key tactic for marketers.

- According to a 2008 study from ExactTarget and Ball State University's Center for Media Design, 18- to 34-year-olds claim they are more likely to be influenced to make purchases based on e-mail marketing messages and direct mail than marketing messages on social networks.

- A 2008 survey by Forrester Research revealed that 95 percent of surveyed marketers use e-mail marketing, with another 4 percent expected to do so by year end.

- In January 2008, Jupiter Research forecasted that spending on e-mail marketing would grow from $1.2 billion in 2007 to $2.1 billion in 2012.

- A study of Irish marketers by Marketing Institute and News Weaver found e-mail marketing is important to Irish marketers and is an essential part of their marketing mix. More than three-quarters, or 78.1 percent, of respondents said that e-mail was either "important" or "very important" to their overall marketing strategy. More than two-thirds, or 68.8 percent, of marketers "always" use e-mail for internal communication, followed by just more than half, or 52.1 percent, who use it for "maintaining customer relationships," and about a third, or 31.8 percent, who use it to increase Web site traffic.

E-mail marketing works for a variety of reasons:

- It allows targeting
- It is data driven
- It drives direct sales
- It builds relationships, loyalty, and trust
- It supports sales through other channels

Advanced methods of e-mail are customized to an individual recipient, and all campaigns sent out generate a huge amount of actionable data to use to refine your approach and messages. E-mail promotions and offers generate immediate action, such as sales, downloads, inquiries, and registrations. Informative e-mail newsletters and other e-mails send buyers to online stores and events, act as a foundation for catalogs, increase awareness, grow branding, strengthen relationships, and encourage trust and further loyalty.

E-mail Tips

- **Do not use "canned" e-mails.** Write your note in the same friendly tone you would use if you were talking face-to-face or over the phone. Start with a friendly "Hello" to establish the positive tone and let the customer know that this is a personal e-mail, directly from the Yahoo! store merchant.

- **Keep your feelings to yourself.** You may be upset about what the customer has said or the problems noted, but that cannot show in your e-mail. Nine times out of ten, if you let the customers know that their comments are appreciated, and you will do anything to be of service, they will back off and may even become friendly.

- **Remember that everything you write is in print.** This is not a telephone conversation. This is actual black-and-white evidence of your comments.

- **Respond to every e-mail — good, bad, or indifferent.** The customer took the time to write the e-mail, so that means it is important. You do not have to send a long response, just enough to let the customer know that you read the comments and your thoughts.

- **Send an e-mail even when you do not have an answer.** Perhaps the customer wants to know when the product will be available again or whether there will be an updated version. Say you will get back as soon as you know, and then keep this in an "active" file, so you can provide the information when available.

- **The Yahoo! e-mail after the sale should be the only form e-mail.** You can use "cut-and-paste" paragraphs for common issues. Begin the e-mail with the personal greeting and use a copy-and-paste response in the middle of the note where standard information is needed. This way, the consumer is already feeling comfortable with the tone, and the standardized answer does not seem out of place. You were able to get out a quick response but made the customer feel good about writing. When someone takes the time to send an e-mail, a canned response is not well received.

- **Do not forget about the telephone.** Sometimes it is much easier talking on the phone than sending e-mails back and forth. In many respects, the phone is a much better medium for communication.

- **Acknowledge the customer's concerns.** Say that you understand the customer's issue, and you want to clear up any misunderstandings or problems. Customers rarely ask for anything that goes beyond their original expectations (which may have differed from yours). There is no need to offer a free gift, which shows you feel guilty, or spend considerable time writing about a small issue, such as a slight packaging error. Simply respond to the concern and fulfill the expectation, if possible. If the customer does not understand the information correctly, offer a choice for a solution. Rather than refunding the entire amount, a compromise can be found if the communication is kept on a positive note.

- **Always follow up and make sure all is well.** Once an issue is resolved, write an e-mail to make sure the customer is satisfied. Advise the customer that you are pleased to be of service and are available whenever any other need arises.

- **Thank the customers for their input.** At the end of all e-mails, tell customers you always like to hear from them. You are starting on a friendly note and ending on one.

- **Keep these responses on file.** They are a good way of seeing trends and information if and when this same customer contacts you with another concern.

CHAPTER 14

Marketing Your Yahoo! Store, Part 3

There are so many marketing and promotional opportunities available to business owners like you that you are only limited by your time, money, and creativity. In this chapter, we will discuss what some of those opportunities are and how you can use those tools and techniques to promote your business. At the end of the discussion, we will explain a simple marketing planning method to help you formulate a marketing and promotions program for your first year in business. Put on your marketing hats — we are ready to roll!

Branding

Branding used to be the latest buzzword in marketing. Although the term is no longer trendy, the concept of branding is in place at virtually every successful company in the world. Branding is the consistent use of a company's "brand" — including style, layout, color, and messaging — throughout all its materials and interactions with external customers and stakeholders. The purpose of branding is to convey the look and feel of a company's brand so frequently and consistently that the brand becomes synonymous with the company itself.

To illustrate the branding concept, consider the following major brands: Coca-Cola, Ford, Nabisco, Wall Street Journal, Pillsbury, and Michelin. When you think of those companies, do you envision their logo or another visual element the company has advertised or promoted? Did you have any trouble conjuring up those images, or did they pop into your head quickly and effortlessly? Without having to put much thought into it, when you see a Coke bottle or a chubby white doughboy, you know what companies these images represent.

In fact, Yahoo! is one of the best stories on branding, which we noted in the introduction. The company name is known worldwide, which has greatly helped expand its business. By having a Web site with Yahoo!, you are piggybacking on Yahoo!'s name and reach and using it as a springboard for your own business name. You can brand your company just as these larger companies, albeit on a smaller scale. First, unless you have some marketing background, you will want to study all the elements of a good branding campaign, or consider consulting with a marketing professional or graphic designer. The elements that you will want to consider when developing your brand are as follows.

Signature Block

Expand your marketing efforts quickly and easily by adding information about your Yahoo! store to your e-mail signature block. Promote your latest product or service, an upcoming sale or special promotion, or simply ask them to visit your Yahoo! store. Here are some examples:

> I Love Antiques and My Fabulous Antique Trains
> 888-555-1111
> **www.iloveantiques.com**

Visit my new online store today for rare antique trains: **www.myfabulousantiquetrains.com!**

Or

Visit **www.myfabulousantiquetrains.com** today and get 15 percent off your next purchase. Coupon code: XYZ123.

Or

Need a unique gift? Visit **www.myfabulousantiquetrains. com** today for gift ideas for that hard-to-shop-for person in your life!

Style

Define your style. It is casual, professional, or kitschy? In other words, what sort of feel do you want potential customers to get when they see your brand? If you are selling urns, for example, you probably want a low-key, sedate style. If you are selling kites and Frisbees, however, you might prefer something light-hearted and fun. If you are selling organizers and planners, a professional style might be more appropriate.

Logo

Now that you know what style bests suits your business, consider creating your own logo with a software program or having a professional logo designed for you. As you develop a logo, try to be open-minded and to think from your target customer's point of view. What would spark your interest and draw you in? Does it have to be a picture of some kind, or can various visual elements (e.g., blocks, curves, lines, and shadows) combine to create something a bit more abstract? If you are not sure where to begin, study your competitors' logos. What attracts your attention? What turns you off? Once you have chosen a logo, put it on everything related to your company — business cards, letterhead, gift certificates, coupons, newsletters, Web site, t-shirts, jackets, sweatshirts, your SUV, pens, and trinkets. Use your logo so often that when potential customers see it, they think of your company automatically.

Company Colors

Choose two or three coordinating colors that will represent your brand. The colors you choose will not only depend on your personal preferences, but also on your style and logo. Are cool colors, such as blues, greens, purples, pinks, and blue-based reds, right for your brand, or are warm colors, such as yellows, oranges, browns, orangey reds, better suited?

Fonts

Some people like to use many different fonts throughout their materials to display their creativity and ingenuity. Rather than exciting readers, however, an overuse of font styles and sizes can be distracting to the eye. It is better to limit yourself to two or three font styles in your written materials, such as you Web site, brochure, and letterhead. Choose a mixture of fonts that suit your business and translate well to the materials where they will be used. Consider the difference between serif fonts (those with embellishments at the end of different strokes) versus sans serif fonts, which are clean, clear characters. Some designers say that serif fonts are easier to read in print, while sans-serif fonts translate better online. Others say that it depends on the layout, and that keeping consistency and type that mixes well is more important. Here are some examples of both types, so you can see the differences:

<u>Serif fonts</u>	<u>Sans serif fonts</u>
Garamond	Arial
Times New Roman	Tahoma
Bookman Old Style	Geneva
Courier New	Verdana

To make sure which type is best, print out your Web site page in serif type and then change it to sans serif. See which one is easier to read. It will depend on the on the other elements of the page, the amount of copy, the type in your headlines, the color, and the visuals.

Tagline or Slogan

A tagline or slogan is a brief phrase or sentence that sums up what your company represents. Used in conjunction with a company's logo and its other branding elements, the tagline or slogan becomes a powerful tool in building your brand and projecting a positive, memorable image.

To create a tagline to promote your business, start by setting aside some time for a brainstorming session. At the top of a piece of paper, write down the name of your business and a brief list of the products and/or services you offer. Next, create a list of words that describe your business. Include nouns, action verbs, and adjectives. To provide an example, let us say that you are opening an online store that sells Ty Beanie products exclusively.

Your brainstorming list might look like this.

Store Name: Beanie Babies Galore

Products Offered	Services Offered
Rare Beanie Babies	Gift wrapping
Beanie Baby Bears	Overnight shipping
Holiday Beanie Babies	Doll repair
Sports-themed Beanie Babies	
Beanie Buddies	
Beanie Kids	
Beanie Baby accessories	
Beth's Beanie Baby Club	
Beth's Beanie Baby Checklist	
New Beanie Babies	
Used Beanie Babies	

Descriptive words

VERBS	
Cuddle	Play
Snuggle	Specialize

NOUNS	ADJECTIVES
Toys	Soft
Stuffed animals	Furry
Dolls	Funny
Club	Cuddly
Checklist	Colorful
Animals	Complete
Bears	Playful
Gifts	Silly
Clothes	Sweet
Furniture	Unique
Love	Rare

Now use this information to brainstorm tagline ideas.

- Beanie Babies Galore — your complete Beanie Baby store!

- Beanie Babies Galore — your complete online Beanie Baby store!

- Beanie Babies Galore — we have all of your Beanie Baby needs covered.

- Beanie Babies Galore — for all your Beanie Baby needs!

- Beanie Babies and more at Beanie Babies Galore!

- Specializing in Beanie Baby toys, dolls, gifts, and more at Beanie Babies Galore!

- Beanie Babies Galore — new, used, rare, and unique Beanie Babies and more!

- New, used, rare, and unique Beanie Babies and more at Beanie Babies Galore

- Shop at Beanie Babies Galore for Beanie Babies, dolls, gifts, and more!

- See what we have in store at Beanie Babies Galore!

- Add a little soft, sweet, furry love to your life at Beanie Babies Galore!

Sometimes a merchant will know the tagline as soon as he or she hears it. Others will contemplate and ruminate for a few days until they are satisfied that they have chosen the right slogan. We suggest choosing one or two slogans that you love, and then setting them aside for a day or two. Share the ideas with a few close friends to get their reactions. What did they think? Did they love the slogan? Hate it? See something in it you had not considered? Were their reactions positive?

When you are satisfied that you have the right slogan, plaster it everywhere — your business cards, your Web site, your letterhead, your e-mail signature, the side of your mini-van — anywhere it will get noticed. Use it in your elevator speeches, your newsletter, and in every ad you place. Make your tagline synonymous with your business. It may never become as well known as "Got milk?" but it can help you to define and promote your business more than you realize.

Advertising

As a merchant with an online store, you will want to promote your business in a variety of ways, including advertising online. This is an evolving concept, however, so what works today may not work six months from now. We recommend testing several online advertising methods, and monitoring and measuring your results regularly. Choose those methods that work best for you.

Advertising online can take a variety of forms, including everything from banner ads and text-only ads to sponsored searches and Google AdWords ads.

CASE STUDY: DAN TROY

Dan Troy
Rock Solid Results
58 Winslow Road
Dunbarton, NH 03046
603-496-3623
www.rocksolidresults.com

"There are several aspects about the Yahoo! store that I like," states Dan Troy, president of Rock Solid Results, a Web site designer and strategist in New Hampshire who has worked with Yahoo! store owners. "The Yahoo! brand is a big advantage — it says credibility and safety." Troy, who started his business in 2002, prides himself on excellent customer service. He teams with many organizations that are new to the e-commerce world, so he does a good deal of personal hand holding. "My strength is truly listening to what my client wants," Troy stresses. Like Yahoo! customer service, he is reached easily by either phone or e-mail, depending on what vehicle the client works with best.

ROCK SOLID RESULTS

Promotions

Promotions can take many different forms, including contests, donations, specials, sales, coupons, discounts, gift certificates, postcards, bag stuffers, event sponsorships, and trade show booths.

It is best to try to plan upcoming promotions when you do your marketing planning for the year. List the types of promotions you want to do, how and when you want to do them, when you will need to begin planning them, and how much each will cost you. Then determine how you will measure your success. For example, if you offer coupons in your e-mail newsletter, your newsletter service will track how many offers were sent out and how many e-mail newsletters were opened. In the weeks and months following the distribution of the newsletter, you can measure the number of sales associated with that coupon code. Then look at how much it cost you to make the offer (cost of e-mail newsletter as well as the coupon's value). Did it bring in new customers? Did you profit on the sales? If the promotion worked well for you, plan to repeat it. If not, try tweaking the promotion to have greater appeal and ROI. If you are certain it was a waste of time and money, cross it off your marketing plan altogether.

Networking — Off and Online

Offline, face-to-face networking within your community remains a powerful marketing tool. Do you belong to any local networking groups? If so, make sure you participate regularly to keep your name in front of potential customers and referral sources. If not, consider joining your local chamber of commerce, downtown association, newcomer's group, or other business-networking group. Many local groups hold meetings specifically for meeting other business owners to talk about what they do.

Often, in addition to attending breakfast and hearing a speaker, chamber meeting participants get to speak about their companies for a minute. Additional networking time follows the meeting for people who want to follow up with individuals they want to meet. Some local downtown associations sponsor informal, monthly networking cocktail hours for downtown and work-at-home businesses to get together. All of the cities in an area, for example, may sponsor a business networking conference. Participating in these functions is a good way to spread news about your Yahoo! store to your local marketplace.

Participating in industry-related groups can also be helpful. Consider attending a meeting or two to see whether the group fits with your goals. If so, join the group and volunteer to fill an active role (e.g., membership chair, greeter, or marketing coordinator). Some industry-specific groups include the Society of Professional Journalists, the American Marketing Association, the National Association of Realtors®, Mothers' Home Business Network, the National Association for the Self-Employed, and the Travel Industry Association.

If time, money, or location prevents you from becoming part of such a group, consider volunteering locally to get to know others in the community. Consider wearing a logo item, such as a t-shirt or sweatshirt, the next time you volunteer at the food pantry, practice with your church choir, or organize your neighborhood garage sale. Donate appropriate products and services during the holiday season. These are also ways for you to interact with like-minded individuals while subtly sharing information about your business.

There are many online forums, associations, and organizations you can belong to, as well. When you establish your niche, you will find the other businesses and online population who are interested in the same topic. You can share ideas and learn from each other. Never feel like you cannot contact a fellow Yahoo! merchant and ask for advice. There are many annual conferences online marketing companies hold. Also, increasingly, you will find webinars and teleconferences that cover information of interest.

Publicity

Publicity — when used properly — can be a good tool to promote your business, sometimes without spending a dime. For the purpose of this discussion, we will confine publicity to the media picking up or producing a story about you or your business. An example would be a local newspaper calling you for an interview after reading a press release about your company's donation of 100 teddy bears to kids whose parents are serving in the military. In this case, you produced and distributed the press release, which may have cost you a few bucks, but the story in the newspaper did not cost anything. We call that free publicity, and, as long as it is positive, it is a good thing.

Other ways to garner publicity involve keeping your local media informed of newsworthy events you are involved in. You can keep the media abreast of your business-related news by establishing a relationship with a local reporter, submitting relevant and timely press releases, or remaining in the public eye by volunteering for local organizations and community events. Your business may be included occasionally as events and organizations are covered by the media.

Publicity can also be leveraged online. By distributing press releases to various online media and press distribution outlets, news about you, your business, and your online store may be featured in an online forum, article, or story, drawing potential customers to your site.

Online Social Networking

The Internet is constantly changing, as anyone who is involved with it knows. First, it was Web sites, then blogs, which continue to be marketing leaders, and now, other social networking vehicles have developed. Social marketing consists of all these things, such as blogging and social networking. It is much more than going online to sell a product. When you are becoming a social marketer, your aim is to get to know your customers and clients in any way you can. Your goal is to become a trusted peer, friend, and expert.

Just look at the history of the Internet in terms of e-commerce. When it first started growing, the stress was on driving people to your Web site. Your goal was to sell product, and the best way to do this was to drive as much traffic as possible. You did not have to offer much, since this vehicle was so new that anything different appeared special. Even linking from one place to another was amazing. That took a few years to get old, and other bells and whistles started being developed. Now, there is another revolution going on.

Every day, there are still millions of people who are seeing the Web for the first time. They are getting their information in other ways, beyond just the tried-and-true search engines. This means that if businesses want to sell to them, they need to reach out in other ways than just putting in the right keywords. It is not that banners, paid ads, AdWords, and commercials do not work. They still do their share of selling, because there are many people continuing to use the traditional communication vehicles. Yet there is another whole population that is more into the social side of things and is interested in blogging, social book-marking, and social networking. These have to become a part of any business' marketing plan to become and remain successful.

MySpace, for example, was once the largest social network on-line, but it started a trend. Now there are a number of other networks that have become more business-oriented, such as Twitter and Facebook. As a merchant, you need to influence a person's ideas and thoughts. One way is by offering high-quality, interesting information and lending yourself out as an expert to answer questions and provide feedback. This is as close to networking and relationship building as one can get in a virtual world.

For example, when you blog or provide information on a social network, you can add video, audio, and music, which enhances your visitors' experience. You are also able to provide places for people to input their own comments, vote, respond to surveys, or enter contests. These are all the things that marketers have been doing for centuries. The Internet is just is a different media — a larger, more complex one.

Social marketing is another way for you to build your business and expand your customer base. Whereas in the early years of the Web, you encouraged people to come to your site in order to sell to them. Now, you actually are forming relationships for the long term with much more being considered than whether they will buy a product. Yet, online social networking is significantly different than in-person networking. Traditionally, networking consisted of handing out business cards at monthly meetings and joining for lunches with a few new business acquaintances.

In the virtual world, social networking instead consists of establishing a worldwide community of individuals who share interests through an online vehicle that gives you the opportunity to regularly communicate with one another using Internet resources and tools. By using the platform and tools at the social networking Web sites, users can easily submit information from blogs and videos, encouraging the interaction of huge amounts of people who are like-minded.

This approach is much more socially open than the anonymous forums and bulletin boards that were once popular. Since MySpace was introduced, social networking has grown exponentially. All businesses, especially virtual ones, need to be reaching out to their customers through these social networking sites. This is particularly the case if their target audience is in the teen to 35-year-old age range.

Brand Management

In the past, brand marketing was normally one way — from the company to its targeted audience. Now, with social marketing, this is rapidly turning into a two-way form of communication. A company that is well-received by the social network often receives "free press." It is becoming increasingly common for people on Twitter and other social networking sites to support a company or complain about service or a product.

This comes as no surprise. It is just an extension of what has been occurring all along with consumers. Traditionally, people would talk to one another when they were considering where to eat or whether to buy that new outfit. Or, when they went into the brick-and-mortar store, they would find one of the clerks and ask what he or she thought about the latest product. With the Internet, people can rate their online vendor as they do on Yahoo!, where millions of other potential buyers can see it. Blog writers tell about their positive or negative thoughts concerning a person or business. According to a study by PowerReviews and Forrester Research, 68 percent of online shoppers read at least four reviews before making a purchase. The social network is the same concept, just wider and faster. Look how quickly the photograph of the airplane in the Hudson River was sent around the world immediately after a Twitter member took a picture and downloaded it onto his site. People were seeing this photograph long before the local press had photos.

The world of marketing as we have known it is changing quickly. The consumer no longer needs to see your advertisement or comments before shopping. They can easily turn to thousands of contacts on their social network and have a quick answer about their intended purchase. A smart businessperson will become a part of this process. If you see something about you or your product on one of the social networks, make your comments. It is a good way to add customers.

Social-Media Sites

Discuss your favorite Web sites with potential customers by uploading and commenting on newsworthy articles. As a member, you can also direct traffic back to your business' Web site.

- **Del.icio.us:** Users organize and publicize interesting items through tagging and networking.

- **Digg:** Members can submit and browse articles in numerous categories, such as technology, sports, and entertainment.

- **Ning:** Create your own network and bring together clients/customers, vendors, and employees.

- **Reddit:** Regularly download items to develop a loyal following and increase your online presence.

- **Squidoo:** Everyone is an expert on something, as you know because of your Web site and product knowledge that you can share with others. Answer questions and help other members.

- **StumbleUpon:** Add a StumbleUpon toolbar to your browser, and find individuals who are interested in your business niche and what you have to say about it.

- **Technorati:** Get more people to visit your blog with this list of blogs and writers in specific categories.

- **Tubearoo:** Extend your media into video and upload tutorials, commentaries, and interviews about your business or industry.

- **WikiHow:** Use the same tutorial for WikiHow on your company's services.

Niche Sites

You have a niche, so share it with others who have the same interest. You can find others in your same industry and consumers who want to know more about your company.

- **BuzzFlash:** Contribute articles on a variety of topics, including your particular niche.

- **HubSpot:** Connect with others in your field through the news of the day.

- **Mixx:** Download stories, rate others, and drive traffic to your site.

- **SEO TAGG:** This is your way to stay abreast of changes in SEO.

- **Small Business Brief:** This is ideal for new small businesses. Just post your e-commerce article, a photo, and a link to your profile to gain exposure and online credibility.

- **Sphinn:** Upload articles and information from your blog to increase interest in your business or interface with others in your industry.

Miscellaneous Sites

The following social-media sites offer excellent marketing opportunities for you to promote your latest news or services.

- **43 Things:** Promote your company's goals and objectives and gain a following of customers, investors, and promoters who cheer you on as you gain success.

- **Newsvine:** Your business is not only made up of products and services, but (maybe) employees who also should be featured here.

- **Wetpaint:** Establish your own social network site to reach your audience and increase your company's presence online.

- **Wikipedia:** Write about areas you know and spread the wealth of knowledge.

- **Yahoo! Answers:** Field Yahoo! users' questions. Search for questions in your particular areas of expertise by clicking various categories. The more you give useful advice and link over to your Web site, the quicker you will gain another new following.

Establishing Credibility with a Blog

The increasing interest in social media does not mean that blogging is disappearing — far from it. Blogging is also a good way to get picked up by the search engines. Short for Web logs, blogs are a combination of an online newsletter, forum, journal, and diary, which revolve around a specific theme related to your Web site. As part of its Web hosting package, Yahoo! offers users the opportunity to create a personal blog. Merchants with Yahoo! stores can also access the Yahoo! 360° blog and activate it on their Web sites. Before setting up your blog, take the following steps:

- Choose a name and description for your blog

- Decide where in your Yahoo! store you want your blog to appear

- Decide what type of content you will include in your blog and how often you will update it

With this information in mind, follow these steps to set up your Yahoo! 360° blog.

1. From the Web Hosting Control Panel, go to the Create and Update tab.

2. Click "Basic Blogging."

3. You will then be asked to choose one of three blogging tools: Yahoo! 360° blog, WordPress, or Movable Type. The latter two options are for more advanced bloggers. For this example, we will choose the Yahoo! 360° blog by clicking on the "Activate" button.

4. Choose between the Standard and Custom options and click on the appropriate button. For this example, we will stick with Standard.

5. Type in a nickname, a blog title, and a description (120 characters maximum).

6. If you want your blog to be your home page, check the box offering that option. We recommend that you leave your storefront as your home page, and allow Yahoo! to place your blog on another page. Click "Next."

7. Review the terms of service and, if you agree, check the box indicated and click on "Activate." Your blog will immediately appear on your Web site. You can add posts to it and announce it to the world right away.

8. After your blog has been created, you will get a welcome message from Yahoo! and can immediately (a) compose and post a blog entry; (b) edit blog settings; and (c) view your blog at the address indicated.

9. To edit your blog settings, click on the appropriate link. Here, you can change the nickname, blog title, and description you originally created. You can also easily create an RSS feed for your blog and add an "Add to My Yahoo!" button.

Besides taking advantage of the support that Yahoo! gives you through its widgets and banners, community building, and sales items, one of the best ways to build online popularity and increase your ratings with the search engines is through these blogs — especially since they are so easy to put together. The main purpose of the blog is to provide relevant, up-to-date information on your established theme. If you sell football jerseys, for example, your blog can have postings on the football season, teams, trading, players, or just your thoughts on certain football issues. Remember, in the minds of your potential buyers, information is one of your most essential products. Offering relevant and up-to-date information:

- Builds community

- Makes you a credible source for visitors

- Keeps people returning to your blog for more information and education

- Encourages visitors to follow your lead with suggested products to buy and go to your Web site and purchase them

- Helps you build customer lists — a must with online marketing

- Gives your visitors an opportunity to become involved with your blog with feedback

- Offers a means of education about your products or services

- Helps you keep the pulse of the users

- Offers relevant material for the search engines

- Enhances your listing rank with the search engines

- Allows you the opportunity to introduce new products

- Sells more of your products

Regardless of whether you use the Yahoo! platform or another blogger template, you will be led step-by-step with some type of tutorial. When you read the instructions on the respective blog platform, you will find all necessary information. It can take as little as 15 minutes to finish up a blog. There will be different templates from which to choose. Blog setups tend to be straightforward and do not require any coding knowledge, which is only necessary once you want to start to personalize your blog and get into more complex design. For your purposes, this will likely be unnecessary. You also have your Web site, which has more of the bells and whistles.

Before you start your blog, you should also spend a few hours traveling online and looking at some of your competitors' blogs for ideas for layout and design, articles, and promotional tools. Also start looking for some blogs that will be appropriate for sharing links. This will begin to expand your audience readership. Just make your blog different enough from everyone else's, and you are on your way.

Patience is crucial when it comes to online marketing. Do not write 20 blog articles on Monday and expect to see them on top of the Google list on Tuesday. It is good to do a few every few days, then give it a few months before you expect to see results. Studies report that there are millions of blogs online, but a large number of these were started and never continued. Another large group never attracted the search engines and are sitting in some online limbo land. Unless you can 1) generate a blog post at least two times a week and 2) continue to do so until you begin to get higher listings on search engines and visitors to the blog, nothing will happen. This can take several months. Too many people do not build up their blog vehicle, because they do not write enough posts or have the patience to wait for responses.

You need a topic that is going to be of interest to your intended visitors and that is related to your product line or theme for your book or Web site. This will take some research, especially for some retailers whose products do not lend themselves to prose. Go back to your initial research and see what your buyers are interested in. It may be a subject that is only somewhat about your merchandise. You have to think carefully about the people you want to target and their interests. Then, you need a subject that you know well, that is wide enough to write about on a regular basis, and that is continually changing and offering something of interest for your readers. Since your blog is about your business, you can write about product industry news you read about in the newspapers, business publications, or online.

Since you need to have a link back to your Web site in the article, your blog post has to relate somehow to the products you are selling. No one is looking for a doctorate-level report on a subject; just a few personal comments can be enough. If you just cannot think of anything for your postings, respond to someone else's blog on a similar topic. Include a link to this other blog in your blog post, and then send the author of that blog an e-mail about the link. This not only provides a topic on which to write, but goodwill with another blogger who already has ratings established. It is quite possible that this blogger will respond by sending a link back to you.

Encourage responses from your own readers. Even ask them to send in articles, and give them top billing. If they are passionate enough about a topic, they will want to write about it. This, too, builds community and lends credibility to both your blog and Web site. Also, it may give you additional blogs and Web sites with which to link. When someone does respond, include a "thank you" on the blog page or send the person an e-mail. After your blog begins to get a following, list it with the blog directories. That will encourage more people to visit and respond and will lead to additional search engine listings. There are thousands of blog directories available for submitting your blogs, and many more directories created daily.

Here again, patience is the key, as you will not be able to register with most of the directories immediately. You have to build up your blog first, since the directories will want a certain number of posts written in your blog before you can be listed. Also, some of the directories are free, and others will charge for their services. Some directories generate little traffic, have many categories and few listings under them, and have low ranking in the search engines. In other words, especially if you are paying to be listed in a directory, make sure you are getting your money's worth. After you sign up with a directory, keep track of the traffic that is or is not being generated, and determine whether the directory is of value.

Here is a list of some of the major blog directories:

1. **Best of the Web Blog Directory** is one of the earliest directories. It is highly selective and accepts blogs that are in existence for six months or more of postings.

2. **Eaton Web Blog Directory** claims to be the oldest such publication. After being listed in this directory, look for an automatic increase in visitors. Each accepted blog is ranked on strength, momentum, and overall content.

3. **Blog Directory / Blog Catalog** is another older listing that has a wide range of categories and allows various searching modes.

4. **Blog Flux** is a directory with a wide variety of categories in alphabetical order. It also offers many useful tools for bloggers.

5. **Blogarama** has more than 80,000 blogs listed with both free and paid listings.

6. **Blogoogle** also has free and paid blog submission. Blogs listed for free must have a specific page rank. They are strict on who they accept, so carefully read the Web site.

7. **Bloggeries** has strong categories and subcategories with a clear, concise layout where readers are able to find their

blogs quickly and efficiently.

8. **Bloggapedia's** home page attracts readers who are interested in top blogs and new posts. There are also different categories from the norm.

The Benefits of Blogs

- Search engines like blogs because they usually have new, up-to-date information. Blogs are designed to reach out to the search engines. The more valuable, solid information you have, the greater the chances for attracting traffic.

- Visitors often would rather read content on a subject that interests them than go to a business product page.

- Content in blogs is picked up by other bloggers, giving you more exposure and traffic.

- People who like the copy on a blog because it is fresh and informative will keep coming back.

- Blogs can create a brand just as easily, if not more easily, than other vehicles. Through the copy content and style, you create an image about yourself and your business.

- You establish relationships with your visitors, who spread the word to others who have similar interests.

- Visitors are looking for credible experts who can answer their questions and help them reach their goals, and your blog can fulfill this need.

- When the time comes to purchase a product, your blog visitors will know where to turn.

Building a Customer List

A blog serves another purpose — growing your customer community. On your blog and Web site, you want to give your visitors an opportunity to sign up for additional information. In order to refrain from any spamming concern, you must first let visitors know exactly what they will receive by "opting in," or agreeing to have their name added to a list. Are they signing up for e-mail notification for sales, monthly e-zines with information about a specific topic related to your product line, weekly e-mail updates, a video, or a free e-book? Give them only what they have agreed to receive. Second, you must promise, and keep the promise, that you will not give or sell their names to any other vendor or service. In a brick-and-mortar business, organizations use advertising, promotions, free giveaways, and contests to develop a list that is used for future marketing purposes.

Online, it is much more difficult to build this list, because there are millions of enterprises and millions of people out in the virtual world. Customer list-building is one of the first things to figure out if you are going to build your online business, since the list — or more specifically, the targeted list — will be the lifeblood of your revenue streams. Many of the reports you receive from Yahoo! will give you specific information about your customers. This is important data to build your business. It will help you break down your lists into specific categories, be they by geography, product, or customer demographic.

Another way of building a list is to write and place articles on the Web with internal links, signatures, or biographical information leading to your blog or Web site. You are building your name recognition and credibility while acquiring names and e-mail addresses. Contributing a weekly article to a number of different specialized article directories offers you an effective way to drive traffic to your product or service. In most article directories, you are allowed to give yourself as the author and add a signature. Usually, you can put a one-line descriptor with your signature and/or Web site address.

Another marketing approach is opt-in e-mail, or sending specialized business electronic mail to recipients who have already approved the receipt of commercial messages. This can be accomplished through services, or "safe lists," where you agree to receive e-mails from other business owners/service providers in exchange for having your own e-mail sent to targeted recipients. The usual opt-in e-mail service permits one post per week.

Similarly, co-registration is when someone refers leads, subscriptions, or memberships with a partner. That is, you and someone with a similar product exchange links and signups on each other's sites. Online, you can find a list of co-registration services offering leads on a fee basis. As with the blog directories, you need to review the sites, determine which may be best for you, and keep track of results.

You can combine your goal of providing information along with building a list. You can offer a weekly e-zine or newsletter, a series of informative e-mails, or an e-book. These offer valuable information, subtly promote your products, and build up a customer list. Your e-book can also be used for many other promotional vehicles. Once you have generated this list, you can use it to keep your name in the forefront of the customer's mind. On a quarterly basis, you can send out specific product news and/or coupons. Repetition — but not spamming — works to sell products or services in the long run, assuming that the individual has given you permission.

On your blog, you can also have a discussion area. Your readers and potential customers can become their own community by being able to write in different topics of interest. There are always provocative or controversial subjects, in addition to informational ones.

CASE STUDY: DAVE JONES

Dave Jones, Co-Owner
www.fundogfred.com

"Yahoo! is ahead of the curve in its infrastructure and remains the most cost effective, with transactions costing less than other e-commerce options. If it not had been for this Yahoo! opportunity, it would have been more difficult to acquire such a variety of tools, such as credit card payment, order management, and ease of uploading images, plus, the best part, it is very user friendly. Yahoo! has a long, well proven track record and a wide community that presents an immediate way to greatly increase your online presence. When you sign up with Yahoo!, you automatically become a part of its vast network of potential customers."

Joining Forums

In addition to starting a blog, you can spread your expertise to other online locations, such as other blogs, message boards, and forums. The important thing to keep in mind is "subtlety." You do not want to join theme-related forums just to promote your products, as this is the easiest way to get thrown out. You can do a search for forums or message boards through Google or any other search engine. For example, if you are selling sugarless candy for diabetics and other individuals who have problems with sugar, you can join forums on diabetic cooking, healthy cooking, sugarless desserts, diabetes, and low blood sugar.

Once you have seen a few forums that appear promising, look at each one and see how many people have been sending messages, the quality of these messages (some forums are just another means for advertising and marketing), and how often people write in. You want a large, active community that is looking for information. Find three of these forums, and then read them for a week or so. Do not write in; get a feel for the forum first in regards to its style and needs. For example, some are more social, while others want more technical information.

When you feel that you understand the culture, respond to some of the comments by offering advice. Do not push your products or services. The more you offer information, the more known you will become, and the more people will come to your site. Your comments may also be picked up by the search engines, depending on the format. When you register, you will be able to include the same signature, or one similar to the one you have at the end of your e-zine articles. You can tailor your signature for the subject of the forum and the people you are targeting. You can also respond to comments made on other blogs. These are seen by all the readers of that blog — an entirely different group of people — and may also be picked up by the search engines.

E-Zines

Electronic magazines, or e-zines, are simply newsletters that are sent out on a regular basis electronically to people who have "opted in" or requested more information from you. You added their name with their knowledge or permission, which is one reason why e-zines are an excellent vehicle for marketing your small business. Your subscribers are actually looking forward to receiving and reading it. They have told you that it is all right for you to send store news, ads, coupons, and information. When you operate a business from a brick-and-mortar store, one of the typical methods of establishing relationships with your customers is greeting your customers as they come in and talking to them a little. Customers enjoy being recognized, especially these days when such communication is rapidly dying out. This helps build trust and establish a relationship with your customers.

On the Internet, this approach naturally cannot work the same way. This does not mean that people like being recognized any less. Anyone who has an online site and sells products or services, regardless of what kind, needs to find ways to build relationships with their potential customers. We talked about blogs and social media, and the e-zine falls into the same category. It is essentially just the blog used in a different format; instead of putting it up online, you are sending it through e-mail. You can post it once it has gone out. If there are relevant articles, they will keep their shelf life for some time. With your e-zine, you can update your customers on information about any new products or the industry. By doing this, you keep them coming back for more.

Your e-zine is another way to establish a trusting relationship with your buyers and potential buyers. You want them to get to know you and learn that they can rely on you and your recommendations. Be there for them if they have questions, if they need advice or support, or if they just want to talk with someone who has more expertise. Your e-zine is much more than an advertisement for your business. It is a connection between you and your readers. E-zine publishing and promotion entails considerable time and effort, but the rewards are well worth it.

Ten E-zine Tips

1. Write the articles yourself rather than using something canned. You have the experience, and your customers want to hear from you. If you have problems writing, just talk into a tape recorder and then have someone transcribe it. There is your article.

2. Include articles about customers who have used your products and their experiences and tips.

3. Do not sell products, but use a case study to explain how you helped a customer or client with a product or service.

4. Use a soft sell by writing a product review about a new item you have in your catalog or a "how to" about a product.

5. Consider side-line articles. If you sell grills, then you can have recipes. If you sell bat houses, write about bats.

6. Have a simple e-book download. This can be a short book on any topic related to your product.

7. Have a Q&A from customers. Look at the e-mails you receive with customer questions.

8. You may have some customers who want to write articles for the e-zine, especially if it gives them some publicity.

9. Always include a feedback box.

10. Have a drawing where customers can win a product.

Yahoo! Marketing Extras

You can also use the other services Yahoo! offers to build your business.

Job Listings

Yahoo! HotJobs (**http://hotjobs.yahoo.com/**) — If you are looking for staff to operate and manage your Yahoo! store, or for temporary help during your busy season, check out Yahoo! HotJobs to post an ad, review resumés, discover hiring solutions, and more.

Downloads

Yahoo! has thousands of free downloadable tools available to users to enhance and customize their Yahoo! experience. These tools might be useful on your Web site or for use in managing your Yahoo! store.

- **Yahoo! Downloads** – Yahoo! offers all its most popular

downloads in one spot: **http://downloads.yahoo.com.** Review the tools and see which ones can increase your productivity or save you a keystroke or two. Tools to try include Toolbars for Mozilla Firefox, Internet Explorer, the Yahoo! edition of Mozilla Firefox and Internet Explorer 7.0, Yahoo! Go for mobile phones, Yahoo! Games, Yahoo! Kids Games, and Music Jukebox.

- **Yahoo! Auto Sync** — Synchronize your address book and calendar between Outlook and Yahoo!, and back-up your critical e-mail addresses to Yahoo! for safekeeping.

- **Yahoo! Messenger** — Use Yahoo! Messenger to communicate instantly with your employees, customers, vendors, family, and friends.

- **Yahoo! Widgets 4.5** — Yahoo! brings you more than 4,000 desktop widgets to choose from so you can stay up-to-date on your favorite sports teams, local weather, stock tickers, desk calendar, day planner, online sticky note/memo pad, system resource monitors, and more.

Online Directories

- **Yahoo! Directories** — Yahoo! offers a wealth of online directories in the following categories (each with its own set of subcategories) and more: Arts and Humanities, Business and Economy, Computers and Internet, Education, Entertainment, Government, Health, News and Media, Recreation and Sports, Reference, Regional, Science, Social Science, Society and Culture, and New Additions in various categories.

- **Yahoo! Local** — As its name implies, Yahoo! Local is a targeted directory that includes business reviews, a directory, maps, a city guide, events, neighborhood buzz, and more. It also includes a "My Local" tab where you can see reviews, collections, recent activity, and recent searches. A Yahoo! Local weekend tab selection tells locals what is going on in their area during the coming weekend.

More Advice and Support

For busy business owners and entrepreneurs, Yahoo! provides a vast amount of advice and information at your fingertips. Here are just some of the many dedicated pages and tools Yahoo! has to offer:

- **Yahoo! Business Tools** — Yahoo! offers a useful collection of business tools in one location, **http://smallbusiness.yahoo.com/r-bizTools**. This page features a small business loan calculator, a business dictionary, and a zip code lookup tool. It also offers package tracking via DHL, FedEx, UPS, and USPS.

- **Yahoo! Help Central** — If you are not sure how to find what you are looking for, Yahoo! Help Central is sure to have an answer for you. As part of the site, users can check out the alphabetical listing of online tutorials for topics such as how to use Yahoo! Mail, Yahoo! Messenger, or Photo Mail. Go to **http://help.yahoo.com/l/us/yahoo/helpcentral** for more information.

- **Yahoo! People Search** — Free white page search for people in the United States or Canada. Just enter the person's first and last name, city, and state at **http://people.yahoo.com** for a phone and address search. You can also search for an e-mail address or phone number. Additional options are available through paid advertisements on the site.

- **Yahoo! Small Business Management and Human Resources** – From Yahoo!'s management and human resources page, **http://smallbusiness.yahoo.com/r-main-Cat-m-5-management_hr-i**, you can access hundreds of useful articles on topics including hiring and recruitment, operations, employment law, employee management, and compensation and benefits.

- **Yahoo! Small Business Finance** – This page, **http://smallbusiness.yahoo.com/r-mainCat-m-2-finance-i**, offers a collection of articles and resources useful to small businesses and new business owners. Subcategories include general advice, accounting, financial management, borrowing, venture capital, taxes, and equity financing.

- **Yahoo! Small Business Getting Started** – This page, **http://smallbusiness.yahoo.com/r-mainCat-m-1-getting_started-i**, offers links to a wealth of resources for small business owners and entrepreneurs. In addition to its featured topics and articles, the page has subcategories including legal, business opportunities, franchises, home business, finance, and business plans. In addition, the page links to videos of real-life success stories from business owners like you.

- **Yahoo! Small Business Legal** – Yahoo! offers useful legal information to small business owners at **http://small-**

business.yahoo.com/r-mainCat-m-4-legal-i. Study up on topics like legal structures, business names, independent contractors, trademark and copyright laws, employment law, and patent and trade law.

- **Yahoo! Small Business Online Business** – Yahoo! offers small business owners dozens of useful topics at its online business page, **http://smallbusiness.yahoo.com/r-mainCat-m-3-online_business-i**. Advice and information on topics like connectivity and access, domains and Web sites, e-commerce, and eBay are just a few clicks away.

- **Yahoo! Small Business Sales and Marketing** – Available at **http://smallbusiness.yahoo.com/r-mainCat-m-6-sales_marketing-i**, this tool allows small businesses to access information about search engines, site design, market research, paid search, branding, lead generation, e-mail marketing, advertising, public relations, and customer service.

Creating Your Yearly Marketing Plan

If you expect to be a million-dollar company in your first year, the marketing planning tips in this book will only serve as the beginning to a long, hard road for you. Assuming you are more of an average entrepreneur, or "netpreneur," we will offer a simple, affordable method for your first year or two of marketing planning.

Some marketing plans are very complicated and take weeks or even a couple of months to develop and refine. However, it is often the case that a much less involved one can be just as effective.

To establish a marketing plan for your company, look at the kinds of marketing you are interested in doing during the upcoming year, for example pay-per-click advertising, an e-mail campaign, development of a new blog or online articles. Then determine the frequency of each of the types of marketing. How often will you send out e-mails? How many months do you plan on doing pay-per-click advertising?

Now you have to determine if you can develop these marketing ideas based on your resources. Do you have the necessary funding and staff to write a new e-zine each month? Do you have the finances to have a special product drawing each quarter? Reduce the list of programs if you have any doubts about meeting your schedule. It is much better to increase your marketing plan than to reduce it, especially if your customers are used to seeing something on a regular basis. Keep the marketing items that will give you the best bang for the buck.

Looking at the remaining items on your list, do you now feel comfortable that you have the staff to meet your expectations? Who will write the blogs or the e-zine if you are unable to do so? Who will get the mailing list finalized? Who will take responsibility for the monthly promotions? If you are alone or have a small staff that may have a problem getting everything done, either hire extra help, or if you have the resources, exchange services with a colleague.

Lastly, be sure to review your marketing plan regularly to determine what needs to be changed or updated. Make your plan flexible enough so that changes can be made if necessary. You will have a better idea of timing, as well, recognizing that certain marketing efforts are better at different seasons, times of the month or days.

Based on this, you can begin to finalize your plans for the rest of the year. What do you hope to accomplish from a marketing perspective? Do you want to grow your customer base, increase revenue, add a new product line, or expand into a different niche market? Write down these general goals and then add specifics about each one. For instance, if you want to grow revenue next year, what amount do you feel is realiastic — 10, 20, or even 100 percent? If you want to add products or a new line, how many products should you add? What kinds? Where will you get them? What will they cost? With your goals in mind, map out a marketing plan month by month. Your plan should include activities with varying frequencies: regular, periodic, and special.

- **Regular activities** are marketing activities that you perform on a frequent or consistent basis. Attending weekly networking luncheons or a monthly chamber of commerce breakfast are examples of regular marketing activities. Sending out an e-mail to existing customers on a monthly basis would also be considered a regular activity.

- **Periodic activities** include marketing activities that you do regularly, but on a less frequent basis — perhaps quarterly or semi-annually. These might include seasonal sales, distribution of press releases, or testing of different online marketing campaigns.

- **Special activities** are those marketing activities that you perform as needed. They might include things like a post-holiday online sale, participating in a local trade show, or getting your Yahoo! store featured in an online magazine.

With your lists of marketing activities in hand, schedule items for each month of the year, noting what date they will occur and how much each activity will cost. This information should also be inserted into your budget. Next, mark the activities you will do no matter what your budget, such as networking meetings and pay-per-click advertising, as well as those that you would like to do if your income permits or to prepare for a particularly slow period — after the holidays, for example. Now assign the tasks. In other words, who will do what? Do you have a staff? If not, the marketing tasks will fall to you. They are often the first to be forgotten when you are successful, but marketing activities should be maintained whenever possible. This is how you get new customers in the door. Reminding them of your value and keeping your name at the top of their mind is often how you keep your customers coming back for more.

Sample Marketing Plan

If you would like to try the simplified marketing planning method, review the following sample plan for my fictitious Yahoo! store, *My Fabulous Antique Trains*.

My Fabulous Antique Trains
Marketing Plan – 2010

Goals
- Grow customer base by 25 percent
- Increase monthly revenue by 10 percent
- Try two new online marketing campaigns

Marketing activities by type and cost

Regular activities:
   Yahoo! pay-per-click marketing campaign (daily) - $150
   Participate in relevant online forums (weekly) - $0
   Local networking luncheon (weekly) - $10
   E-mail postcard announcing monthly specials (monthly) - $10
   Attend local chamber of commerce marketing roundtable (monthly) - $15
   Update blog every week - $0

Periodic activities:
   E-mail newsletter to subscribers (quarterly) - $10
   Press releases (two to four times per year, depending on newsworthy items) - $200
   Quarterly drawing for product - $200

Special activities:
   Annual post-holiday sale (January) - $500 for advertising
   Participate in antique toy trade show (September) - $250 booth fee, $200 for marketing materials
   Seek free publicity for antique train donation to local children's organization (December) - $0
   Chamber of commerce membership - $350/year

2010 Marketing Calendar

<u>January</u>
Daily - Yahoo! pay-per-click marketing campaign
Weekly - Update blog
Tuesdays - Participate in relevant online forums, such as Yahoo! Groups

Thursdays - Local networking luncheon
Annually - Renew chamber of commerce membership
1st - Advertise annual post-holiday sale, both online and in local publications
15th - E-mail postcard announcing monthly specials

February
Daily - Yahoo! pay-per-click marketing campaign
Weekly - Update blog
Tuesdays - Participate in relevant online forums, such as Yahoo! Groups
Thursdays - Local networking luncheon
15th - E-mail postcard announcing monthly specials

March
Daily - Yahoo! pay-per-click marketing campaign
Weekly - Update blog
Tuesdays - Participate in relevant online forums, such as Yahoo! Groups
Thursdays - Local networking luncheon
15th - E-mail postcard announcing monthly specials
25th - E-mail newsletter to subscribers (via newsletter service or using Yahoo! Groups/Lists)

April
Daily - Yahoo! pay-per-click marketing campaign
Weekly - Update blog
Tuesdays - Participate in relevant online forums, such as Yahoo! Groups
Thursdays - Local networking luncheon
1st - Investigate one new online marketing campaign and implement for a two-month period

15th - E-mail postcard announcing monthly specials

<u>May</u>
Daily - Yahoo! pay-per-click marketing campaign
Weekly - Update blog
Tuesdays - Participate in relevant online forums, such as Yahoo! Groups
Thursdays - Local networking luncheon
15th - E-mail postcard announcing monthly specials

<u>June</u>
Daily - Yahoo! pay-per-click marketing campaign
Weekly - Update blog
Tuesdays - Participate in relevant online forums, such as Yahoo! Groups
Thursdays - Local networking luncheon
15th - E-mail postcard announcing monthly specials
25th - E-mail newsletter to subscribers (via newsletter service or using Yahoo! Groups/Lists)

<u>July</u>
Daily - Yahoo! pay-per-click marketing campaign
Weekly - Update blog
Tuesdays - Participate in relevant online forums, such as Yahoo! Groups
Thursdays - Local networking luncheon
15th - E-mail postcard announcing monthly specials

<u>August</u>
Daily - Yahoo! pay-per-click marketing campaign
Weekly - Update blog

Tuesdays - Participate in relevant online forums, such as Yahoo! Groups

Thursdays - Local networking luncheon

15th - E-mail postcard announcing monthly specials

September

Daily - Yahoo! pay-per-click marketing campaign

Weekly - Update blog

Tuesdays - Participate in relevant online forums, such as Yahoo! Groups

Thursdays - Local networking luncheon

1st - Press release to announce participation in upcoming antique toy trade show

15th - E-mail postcard announcing monthly specials

20th - Contact local community newspaper about doing a story on upcoming antique train donation

25th - E-mail newsletter to subscribers (via newsletter service or using Yahoo! Groups/Lists)

October

Daily - Yahoo! pay-per-click marketing campaign

Weekly - Update blog

Tuesdays - Participate in relevant online forums, such as Yahoo! Groups

Thursdays - Local networking luncheon

1st - Investigate one new online marketing campaign and implement for a two-month period

15th - E-mail postcard announcing monthly specials

November

Daily - Yahoo! pay-per-click marketing campaign

Weekly - Update blog

Tuesdays - Participate in relevant online forums, such as Yahoo! Groups

Thursdays - Local networking luncheon

15th - E-mail postcard announcing monthly specials

25th - Mail flyers to existing customers

December

Daily - Yahoo! pay-per-click marketing campaign

Weekly - Update blog

Tuesdays - Participate in relevant online forums, such as Yahoo! Groups

Thursdays - Local networking luncheon

1st - Press release to announce donation of antique train to local children's organization

15th - E-mail postcard announcing monthly specials

26th - E-mail newsletter to subscribers (via newsletter service or using Yahoo! Groups/Lists)

Marketing Strategies for Success

The key to your success will be actually following the plan, adhering to your goals, and making adjustments as needed. Here are some additional strategies to ensure your success:

1. **Choose marketing activities that make sense for your business.** The marketing activities you decide to implement will vary depending on the type of business you have. If you have an online Yahoo! store only, you will want to focus your marketing efforts online with such approaches as e-mail marketing, pay-per-click advertising, SEO, and social bookmarking. If you have a brick-and-mortar establishment in addition to your Yahoo! store, you will want to

do some local marketing as well (e.g., networking groups and joining your local chamber of commerce or downtown association). Make adjustments if some marketing activities yield a better return on your investment than others.

2. **Create a flexible marketing schedule by planning around your busiest times.** If your Yahoo! store receives many orders on Mondays and Fridays, for example, plan your marketing activities on other days of the week. You can also prepare mailings ahead of time when business is slower.

3. **Be consistent.** Whether you decide to send an e-mail newsletter using Yahoo! or another online service, send it out the same day each month or quarter. Customers will get used to the regularity and look forward to receiving your mailings. If you think they will not notice if you skip one, believe it.

4. **Try new marketing techniques** including pay-per-click advertising, online business directories, audio clips, webinars, podcasts, and video product demonstrations. In the online world, new marketing techniques are developing every day, and to keep up with today's tech-savvy customers, you need to stay abreast of changing technology. Give customers what they want by reaching out to them in new ways.

5. **Invest in yourself.** Marketing a new business can be expensive, but it does not have to be. To learn about affordable marketing strategies, invest in "how to" books, do some research on the Internet, attend a community college

class on marketing your small business, or network with other online merchants. It will be time and money well spent.

CASE STUDY: SHAWNA FENNEL

Shawna Fennell, Owner
1 Choice 4 Your Store
2043 South Bend Avenue #135
South Bend, IN 46637
888-312-7839
www.1choice4yourstore.com

Nine years ago, Shawna Fennell began building Yahoo! stores, and her business has been growing ever since. Going into Web site consulting was a logical step. She could use her creative side and help customers at the same time. She knew she wanted to be involved with computers, "because I could foresee in the future that computers would inevitably become more and more involved in our daily lives," she recalls.

As sales picked up, Fennell knew it was time to invest money back into her business. The first step was a new design. The basic Yahoo! Store was good for a start, but she wanted a more professional look and feel to portray to customers. Her store was seriously lacking SEO. Although she had taken courses in Web design, the Yahoo! store uses a language called RTML. There was not much documentation on this language, so she learned RTML and began making changes to her site that increased sales. "I also learned how to reach 'Number 1' in the search engines," Fennell says.

Once her first store was finished, Fennell quickly designed and optimized a second store with a totally different product. Then she designed a third store. "I spent time researching every tiny detail that went into running a Yahoo! store.

CASE STUDY: SHAWNA FENNEL

Although there was good information out there, none of it was specific to the Yahoo! store owner," Fennell states. Then she was contacted by another client, and another, and another.

"Consistently update your Web site with fresh new content. Remember that content is king, and relevancy is queen!"

"That is when the idea came to me: There are other Yahoo! store owners who need one place to go for information on building traffic and making their site look more professional, as well as other aspects of the business, like merchant companies, affiliate programs, press releases, and so much more. Since these Yahoo! owners are already acting as secretary, customer service office, bookkeeper, shipping manager, marketing director, and complaint department, they have their hands full! So, I decided to share my experiences and skills, and 1 Choice 4 Your Store was born. The best part was offering these services at one-third the cost of the 'other guys' who were in the field at the time."

Business boomed. Seventy percent of her business came from referrals and return customers, as it does today. It was time to hire help. She hired several work-at-home moms and dads across the U.S., including her own mother, who joined in 2006. Now she has an additional 15 employees, but continues to keep costs low. "Since we started helping other Yahoo! store owners, we have had the pride and pleasure to watch their sales increase by 200 percent to upwards of 500 percent!"

CASE STUDY: SHAWNA FENNEL

She has clients that own national chains and newbies. "For the brand new store owner, we offer several ways of learning: They read our Yahoo Store Editor 101 e-book, watch our video tutorials, or give us a call, and we can walk them through the Yahoo Store." What tips does Fennell have for Yahoo! merchants? "Focus on SEO. At one time, I was paying over $6,000 a month for advertising. Once I focused on SEO, I decreased that to $500 a month. However, my sales went up. This means my profit went up as well. Content makes up over 80 percent of how your Web site will rank in the search engines. Make sure your product descriptions are unique and relevant to what people search for. Consistently update your Web site with fresh new content. Remember that content is king, and relevancy is queen!"

CHAPTER 15

Yahoo! Just Keeps Going

Throughout this book, you have seen how Yahoo! will work hand-in-hand with you to establish and grow your business for increased income over the years. It takes hard work, but the million-dollar stores that started from scratch know it is well worth it, as do the brick-and-mortar businesses, home-office parents, and the niche lovers.

Hardly a day goes by that Yahoo! does not have something different to announce that will further improve the small business owner's world. Like all successful online companies, it is continually upgrading, changing, and innovating. Case in point, Yahoo! now has a new analytic tool that the business owners love. There had been considerable buzz about this for some time, so no one was surprised that they developed this tool, only that that they did not do it sooner. Google has had its analytic vehicle out for some time.

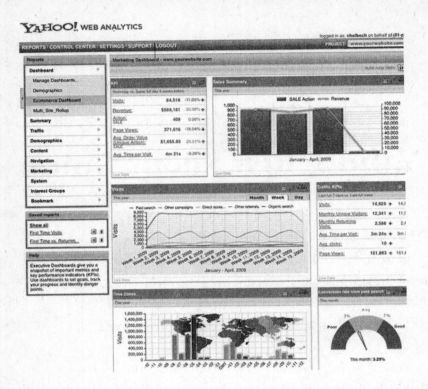

Reproduced with permission of Yahoo! Inc. ® 2009 by Yahoo! Inc. Yahoo! and the
Yahoo! Logo are trademarks of Yahoo! Inc.

One of the major changes taking place on the Internet is the increasing ability to determine how buyers are going to respond. For years, much of Internet marketing has been a hit-and-miss approach. When something worked, everyone went chasing that approach until something else came along. Analytics is putting science and statistics into the equation.

Yahoo!'s Web Analytics is a powerful enterprise site tool that offers real-time insight into how visitors are responding to Web sites. It provides merchants with detailed real-time reporting within minutes after an action occurs on their site, so that sellers can quickly identify dips in key site metrics or monitor the performance of new content. This will considerably help online marketers and Web site designers determine the best way to enhance the visitors' experience, increase sales, and reduce marketing costs.

This tool lets you know what is taking place on your Web site by answering questions such as "How successful are you at attracting valuable visitors?" This goes well beyond counting how many times people click on your search engine listing or keyword. When someone comes to your site, what do they do next? Where do they go? How quickly can they find what they want to see or accomplish what they planned? This information gives you the ability to measure the impact of your Web site design and development. The amazing aspect is you can just change one parameter, and it can make all the difference in whether people buy.

Do your potential customers look for the product information? Do they put things in their shopping carts? And, if so, do they actually buy the product or, as in most cases, leave the site before buying? Do they use the online customer care tools and services? All these questions can now be answered, depending on the level of sophistication of the analytics.

For example, determining how your customers found your site is not difficult. On the other hand, suppose you want to compare the individuals who purchased a product over a period of several weeks against the path they took through your site and the time of day they showed up. Further, you would like to know how many people came from the same source, such as a banner ad, SEO, or a press release, for example. This is much more complicated, since there are several things happening here, each affecting the other.

If you want to know how your Web site is attracting business and responding to its existing customers, this is where analytics comes into play. It is much more sophisticated than a simple traffic counter. Web site analysis tools can track the myriad ways people use your Web site, while making sense of the mountain of data your site generates.

Using these tools, you can find out:

- How many people visited your site, how many returned, and how often?

- How were these users navigating through your site?

- Where is the roadblock in the conversion process? Why do they appear that they are going to buy and then change their minds?

- What content are your visitors looking for, and are they finding it?

- What is driving people away from your site rather than bringing them in?

Site analytics differs from Web site optimization, which makes sure your site is user-friendly.

Web site analysis instead tracks the way visitors use your site, either through analyzing traffic logs after the fact or by tracking requests in real-time as they come in. The former is the older technique. You install software that goes through the raw traffic data your server collects. It organizes it and lets you view the results as bar charts, graphs, or tables. This basic data includes, for instance:

- Number of page requests by date or time
- Requests by browser type
- Requests by operating system
- Referring URLs
- Originating countries
- Status codes (e.g., Successful or Page Not Found)

The new approach observes the traffic as it comes in. You add some code to your page, depending on how your site is organized and the sophistication of the analytics software. Yahoo! store owners have been quite successful already in terms of meeting their customers' needs, which means extra sales and income. With these analytic tools, it just becomes easier.

Analytics is only the latest offering that Yahoo! has provided to the store merchants. More is to come, as always. Since it first established its small business services, Yahoo! has helped thousands of merchants build from small online shops to e-commerce successes making hundreds of thousands, and even millions, of dollars. It is a true team effort. Merchants need a product that can be marketed online, a reliable source for that product, a plan that determines the price to charge to make a profit, and the marketing approach to get people to their site and into a long-term relationship. Yahoo! provides the respected vehicle, platform, and support required to continually go onto the next levels of success. Then, it is up to you to leverage all that Yahoo! has provided and go to the next steps for success.

CASE STUDY: MICHAEL WHITAKER

Founder, Michael Whitaker
Monitus LLC
P.O. Box 1714
Mill Valley, CA 94942
1-415-868-4630
www.monitus.net

Yahoo! store owners need to be familiar with the Internet, running a business, designing Web sites, and managing a wealth of data, from product catalogs and shipping and tax tables to order information and statistics. This is where Monitus offers its help. "With the use of technologies such as Perl, PHP, JavaScript, XML, and MySQL to interface with your Yahoo! Store, we help you run things more efficiently by automating processes and performing advanced data manipulation," explains company founder Michael Whitaker.

In 2001, when he was a general manager of a small European software company based in San Francisco, Whitaker considered what would be the best business to start with his background in engineering and economics. He recognized that there were a number of vendors offering Web design support, so he decided to take a more analytical route.

"Our goal is to help you along the way by focusing on things that increase your conversion rate and drive more traffic to your site. We strive to make your Yahoo! Store more usable and search-engine friendly, and provide you with time-saving order-processing tools," Whitaker explains.

He began helping Yahoo! vendors when asked to select an appropriate e-commerce platform for a company opening an online store.

CASE STUDY: MICHAEL WHITAKER

"Before I even got involved with the Yahoo! Store platform, I recommended the Yahoo! Store over an expensive, custom-built solution," Whitaker recalls. "I started customizing more and more Yahoo! stores, and also writing books and giving seminars on the topic."

"If you do a redesign or implement a new feature in your Yahoo! Store, Web analytics data can tell you if this has affected the conversion rate."

Whitaker focuses specifically on e-commerce sites, because it is actually possible to measure whether an online site works or not. "If you do a redesign or implement a new feature in your Yahoo! Store, Web analytics data can tell you if this has affected the conversion rate. We have developed a number of analytics tools specifically for the Yahoo! Store platform that are designed to give merchants actionable data, such as the best keywords to target in marketing campaigns or how to reduce shopping cart abandonment." According to various studies, online shoppers abandon 50 percent to as much as 75 percent of all carts. This is better known as "shopping cart abandonment." There are many reasons why shopping cart abandonment rates are so high, and certain techniques can recover some of these lost sales.

"Sometimes all it takes to convert a visitor into a new customer is just some extra help, assurance, or a little incentive. Our unique shopping cart recovery service enables merchants to get in touch via e-mail with visitors who have not completed the checkout process," notes Whitaker. Monitus will set up this shopping cart recovery service for free, and only charges a typical affiliate commission for successfully recovered carts.

List of Yahoo! Services

Millions of users, including small business owners and entrepreneurs, turn to Yahoo! every day for its wealth of offerings. While not all Yahoo! ventures have been successful — some, like Auctions and Bill Pay, have been discontinued — many remain alive and well in the world of Yahoo!.

- My Yahoo! — personalize your Yahoo! experience with a customized Yahoo! home page

- Yahoo! Address Book — get a free online address book with a free e-mail account

- Yahoo! Autos (**http://autos.yahoo.com**) — new and used car prices, reviews, and more

- Yahoo! Buzz Index (**http://buzz.yahoo.com**) — ranks topics users are searching for online

- Yahoo! Calendar — an online calendar to help you stay organized

- Yahoo! Careers (**http://careers.yahoo.com**) — a career resource and job search center

- Yahoo! Classifieds (**http://classifieds.yahoo.com**) — free Yahoo! classifieds, including Autos, HotJobs, Real Estate, Rentals, Tickets, and Personals (For Sale and Pets categories are no longer available)

- Yahoo! Companion (**http://toolbar.yahoo.com**) — customizable Yahoo! toolbar

- Yahoo! Company Store (**http://companystore.yahoo. com**) — if you are a huge fan of Yahoo!, you will want to browse its online store for trinkets and gadgets (you have to see the yodeling can opener)

- Yahoo! Digital (**http://digitalhome.yahoo.com**) — Yahoo! on your TV

- Yahoo! Entertainment (**http://entertainment.yahoo. com**) — celebrity news, gossip, music videos, games, and more

- Yahoo! Finance (**http://finance.yahoo.com**) — stock quotes, financial news, investments, and more

- Yahoo! Food (**http://food.yahoo.com**) — recipes, restaurants, and more

- Yahoo! Games (**http://games.yahoo.com/games/front**) — online games

- Yahoo! Go 3.0 (**http://mobile.yahoo.com/go**) — take Yahoo! with you wherever you go

- Yahoo! Greetings (**http://www1.yahoo.americangreetings.com/index.pd**) — online greeting cards through American Greetings

- Yahoo! Groups or Yahoo! Clubs (**http://groups.yahoo.com**) — join or create a Yahoo! group to connect with like-minded individuals and groups

- Yahoo! Health (**http://health.yahoo.com**) — information on wellness, diet and fitness, conditions and diseases, and more

- Yahoo! HotJobs (**http://hotjobs.yahoo.com**) — online job searches, resumé builder, and career tools

- Yahoo! Kids Games (**http://kids.yahoo.com/games**) — online games for kids

- Yahoo! Mail (**http://mail.yahoo.com**) — free Web mail service

- Yahoo! Maps (**http://maps.yahoo.com**) — maps, driving directions, and traffic information

- Yahoo! Merchant Solutions and Small Business Center (**http://smallbusiness.yahoo.com**) — online solutions for small businesses and retailers

- Yahoo! Message Boards (**http://messages.yahoo.com**) — online forums for various topics, including business and finance, computers and Internet, and government and politics

- Yahoo! Messenger (with voice), also called Yahoo! Chat (**http://messenger.yahoo.com**) — download Yahoo!'s instant messenger to chat live with your friends

- Yahoo! Movies (**http://movies.yahoo.com**) — check out movie reviews, show times, and trailers

- Yahoo! Music Unlimited (**http://new.music.yahoo.com**) — Internet radio, music videos, artists, news, and more

- Yahoo! News (**http://news.yahoo.com**) — top news headlines

- Yahoo! Personal Finance (**http://finance.yahoo.com/personal-finance**) — a subcategory of Yahoo! Finance focusing on individuals with categories such as retirement and credit

- Yahoo! Podcasts (**http://audio.search.yahoo.com/audio**) — search for your favorite podcasts using this audio search feature; features music, news, lectures, and more

- Yahoo! Real Estate (**http://realestate.yahoo.com**) — search for homes for sale, mortgage information, and more

- Yahoo! Search (**http://search.yahoo.com**) — one of the Web's most popular search engines

- Yahoo! Shopping (**http://shopping.yahoo.com**) — shop at more than 72,000 online Yahoo! stores for everything from clothing and home and garden products to toys and outdoor gear

- Yahoo! Small Business (**http://smallbusiness.yahoo. com**) — see Yahoo! Merchant Solutions

- Yahoo! Sports (**http://sports.yahoo.com**) — news, scores, fantasy games, and more

- Yahoo! Travel (**http://travel.yahoo.com**) — travel information including a travel guide, trip planner, FareChase, deals, and more

- Yahoo! TV (**http://tv.yahoo.com**) — TV listings, videos, photos, news and gossip, and online TV episodes

- Yahoo! Upcoming (**http://upcoming.yahoo.com**) — a

social event calendar that allows users to post and search ofr upcoming events

- Yahoo! Video (**http://video.yahoo.com**) — contains videos users can upload and share

- Yahoo! Wallet (**http://wallet.yahoo.com**) — store all your credit card information online for shopping for easy checkout

- Yahoo! Weather (**http://weather.yahoo.com**) — forecasts, weather maps, news, and features

- Yahoo! Widgets (**http://widgets.yahoo.com**) — miscellaneous Yahoo!-friendly online tools for your desktop

- Yahooligans! (for kids)

Bibliography

Angel, Karen. *Inside Yahoo! Reinvention and the Road Ahead*. New York: Wiley, 2002.

Bausch, Paul. *Yahoo! Hacks: Tips & Tools for Living on the Web Frontier*. Sebastopol, CA: O'Reilly, 2005.

Davenport, T.H. and J.G. Harris. *Competing on Analytics; The New Science of Winning*. Cambridge, MA: Harvard Business School Press, 2007.

Harper, Stephen C. *McGraw-Hill Guide to Starting your Own Business*. New York: McGraw Hill, 2003.

Kent, Peter. *How to Make Money Online with eBay, Yahoo! & Google*. New York: McGraw Hill, 2006.

Rognerud, Jon. *Ultimate Guide to Search Engine Optimization*. New York: Entrepreneur Press, 2008.

Small Business Administration. **www.sba.gov**

Strange, Carol Anne. *How to Start and Run an Internet Business*. Oxford, UK: How Too Books, 2007.

Yahoo! Small Business **www.smallbusiness.yahoo.com**

Y Store Blog. **http://ystoreblog.com/blog**

Glossary of Terms

The following is of a list of general business, marketing, and technology terms throughout the book.

An entirely new vocabulary has developed from the Internet in a little more than a decade. Before proceeding into the virtual world of online selling, it is important to become acquainted with these new terms.

- **Affiliate:** A typical term for one Web site that drives traffic to another in exchange for a percent of sales from users attracted to the site. Amazon refers to its affiliates as "Associates."

- **Analytics/Web analytics:** A tool that measures the impact of a Web site on its users. E-commerce organizations frequently rely on analytics software to create reports on measures, including how many visitors were converted to buyers or were unique to the site, how they arrived at the Web site, which keywords were entered into the site's search engine, the length of time they stayed on a page or the entire site, the links they clicked on, and when the visitors left the site.

- **Address Verification Service (AVS):** Used by merchant banks and merchant account holders to confirm that a customer's order address is the same as his or her credit card billing address.

- **Bid:** The maximum amount you are willing to pay per click or per performance in a keyword or other online marketing campaign.

- **Berkeley Software Distribution (BSD):** Refers to Unix-like operating systems.

- **Blog:** Comes from web log; a journal that is available on the web. To update a blog is "blogging," and someone who keeps a blog is a "blogger." New blogs tend to be written every day on a site created by software that is easy to use and maintain, even without much technical knowhow.

- **Brick(s)-and-mortar:** A company or a shop that has a physical, rather than a virtual, presence.

- **Category targeting:** Delivery of a specific message to categorized Web sites to reach users most likely interested in products or services being offered in order to increase the effectiveness of a marketing campaign.

- **Click-through rate (CTR):** The rate at which visitors click on a product advertisement. To measure CTR, the number of users who clicked on an ad is divided by the number of times the ad is delivered.

- **Conversion:** The percentage of how many products are shipped divided by the number of clicks on a Web site link. If a Web site gets 200 clicks, and those referrals generated 18 shipped items, the conversion rate would be 18/200=0.09, or 9 percent.

- **Cross-selling:** Offering similar merchandise to a customer who previously bought one product in order to encourage that person to make another similar purchase.

- **Card Verification Value (CVV):** The three-digit code on the back of a credit card. The credit card issuer uses this code to validate the status of the cardholder.

- **Doing Business As (DBA):** A business name that is different from your own name.

- **Domain name:** The unique identification of a Web site. Domain names always have two or more parts separated by dots.

- **Domain name system (DNS):** Converts Internet domain names into Internet protocol numbers. A DNS server performs this kind of translation.

- **E-commerce/electronic commerce:** A methodology used for executing business on the Web or for the online shopping industry.

- **Electronic mail (E-mail):** Usually text, sent from one person to another through the computer.

- **Employer Identification Number (EIN):** Federal Tax Identification Number used to identify a business entity.

- **E-tailer:** A firm that buys products and resells them online, just as traditional retailers do offline.

- **Extensible Markup Language (XML):** A general-purpose specification for creating custom markup languages.

- **File Transfer Protocol (FTP):** This is the easiest and most secure method for exchanging files over the Internet. An FTP Client is software for transferring files between two computers via the Internet. The software must be installed on your computer and only used with a live connection.

- **Frequently Asked Questions (FAQs):** Information added to your Web site that helps customers with the questions they often ask.

- **Home page:** Traditionally, this was the Web page that the browser is set to use when it starts up. Also, it is the main Web page for a business, organization, person, or collection of Web pages.

- **Hyperlinks (links):** Hypertext connections between Web pages.

- **HyperText markup language (HTML):** The coding language that tells the Web browser how to display a Web page's words and images.

- **Hypertext Transfer Protocol (HTTP):** A set of rules for the transfer of files on the Internet. It also provides a standard for Web browsers and servers to communicate.

- **Impressions:** Number of times that the links are viewed by users.

- **Internet:** Networks that are interconnected using protocols. The Internet connects hundreds of thousands of independent networks across the globe. The World Wide Web, or Web, provides a means of accessing information over the Internet.

- **Internet protocol (IP):** The manner or "protocol," by which data is transferred from computer to computer on the Internet. Every computer on the Internet, also called the host, has at least one IP address that specifically differentiates it from any other computer on the Internet.

- **Java:** An Internet-based programming language that creates applications that run while you are online, using your Web browser. Yahoo! PageBuilder is a Java-based application.

- **JPEG (Joint Photographic Experts Group):** A means of compressing visuals so they can be more easily sent from one computer to the next.

- **Linux:** An operating system that is distributed freely and used for both personal and work computer operations. It was developed by Linus Torvalds.

- **Limited Liability Company (LLC):** Similar to a corporation, owners have limited personal liability for the debts and actions of the LLC, but like a partnership, the LLC provides management flexibility and the benefit of pass-through taxation.

- **Keyword:** A word or phrase that sums up the essence of your Web site or other online copy, which is used to attract online search and target advertising. Advertisers buy keywords on search engines to market their site information.

- **Merchant account:** An Internet bank account that a site requires to receive electronic payments.

- **Meta tag:** "Meta" means "about this subject." This consists of information that a visitor does not see on the Web site, but rather is used to provide search engines with an easier way to categorize the contents of a page.

- **Navigation:** This online feature allows users to move from one place to another by clicking on links in a menu bar.

- **Netpreneur:** a newly created term denoting an online or Internet entrepreneur.

- **Online store:** A business-to-customer or business-to-business virtual e-commerce Web site that features and sells merchandise or services.

- **OrderMotion:** A software integration tool that assists small- and medium-sized merchants with their back-office functions, including order capture and processing, inventory management, and payment processing.

- **PayPal:** A leader in facilitating safe online payments via credit cards, bank accounts, buyer credit, or PayPal account balances. Used as an option for customer payments for Yahoo! merchants.

- **Pay-Per-Click:** A means for driving traffic to a Web site using search engine advertising; it is necessary to pay only when someone visits the designated Web site.

- **PHP:** An open source, server-side, HTML-embedded scripting language used to create dynamic Web pages.

- **POP or POP3:** A standard protocol for receiving e-mail; e-mail is received and held by a server for you to download periodically.

- **Relevance ranking:** The measure of how well the indexed page answers the search query when there are a large number of matches to that question.

- **Return on investment (ROI):** A means to evaluate a financial plan.

- **RSS Feeds:** These are live feeds; as the action or show is playing, one is able to add them to the home page.

- **SCORE:** A volunteer organization comprised of business executives who offer free advice and consultations to budding business owners.

- **Search engine:** A Web-based system for searching information available on the Web, such as Google, MSN, Yahoo, and Ask.

- **Search engine marketing:** A set of marketing methods,

often involving paid ads, designed to increase the visibility of a Web site in search engine results pages, such as Google.

- **Search engine optimization (SEO):** The practice of designing Web pages so that they rank as high as possible in search engine results.

- **Seller:** Whoever fulfills the order.

- **Shopping cart/shopping basket:** Online merchants use this software to help visitors add items to their cart after making a purchase. When they are ready to check out, the software adds the total price for the order, including shipping and handling.

- **Simple Mail Transfer Protocol (SMTP):** Transfers e-mail across the Internet

- **SpamGuard:** A guard against mass or repeating e-mails, or e-mails that are received that are not listed in a safe address list (address book).

- **SWOT:** A business analysis tool that helps users define their strengths, weaknesses, opportunities, and threats.

- **Targeting:** The use of advertisements that are designed to appeal to users who fit a particular marketing delineation.

- **Tracking:** Online, real-time reporting to measure the impact of advertisements on users.

- **Transaction:** The act of purchasing a product or service from an e-commerce Web site.

- **Web site traffic:** The number of visitors that view a Web site.

- **Uniform Resource Locator (URL):** A Web page address. The beginning of the address is the protocol identifier, and the end specifies the IP address and the domain name.

- **Unique visitors:** In Web marketing, individuals who have visited a Web site or received specific content, such as ads or e-mail, for a specified period of time, such as a day or month.

- **Unique Selling Proposition (USP):** A company's unique selling proposition is the factor or factors that differentiate a company and its products and services from its competitors.

- **Unix:** A multi-user operating system to create most programs and protocols that built the Internet.

- **Uniform Resource Locator (URL):** The address of a Web page.

- **U.S. Small Business Administration (SBA):** Part of the U.S. government that provides support to small businesses.

- **Web crawler:** An electronic "robot" that connects to interacting computer systems and also compiles an index of links to documents.

- **Web page:** A document created to be viewed in a Web browser.

- **Web site:** The entire number of Web pages and other information, such as images, sound, and video files that are located at the same Internet location.

- **World Wide Web (or Web):** A network of interlinked hypertext documents accessed through the Internet.

About the Authors

After 20 years in the corporate world, author Dana Blozis started Virtually Yourz, her own writing, editing, and marketing company. In addition to working for small businesses, nonprofits, and municipalities, Blozis writes for publication. Her work has appeared in The Seattle Times, Seattle Metropolitan, South Sound magazine,  Computer Source Magazine, The Business Report, Renton and Kent magazines, and more. She lives in Washington State with her family.

This book would not have been possible without the unconditional support of my family, particularly Jim and Brooke. Thank you for your infinite patience and encouragement. – Dana Blozis

During her years as a communication consultant for nonprofit and business clients, Sharon L. Cohen watched and appreciated the rise of the Internet as it affected and changed the world. Once spending most of her time publishing print marketing and information materials and books for nonprofit organizations and corporations, she now communicates online to  complete writing projects for businesses, offer grammatical and literary advice to students, interface with newfound associates and old friends worldwide, and find answers to arcane research questions with several Google clicks. With a passion for writing and reading, she has spent many a day visiting and working in libraries and perusing and ordering books from Amazon. She continues to watch with appreciation the way the Internet may be used to enhance world communication and shared learning and bring education and literacy to the global village.

Cohen is also the author of *Amazon Income: How Anyone of Any Age, Location, and/or Background Can Build a Highly Profitable Online Business with Amazon* and *199 Internet-Based Businesses You Can Start with Less than One Thousand Dollars: Secrets, Techniques, and Strategies Ordinary People Use Every Day to Make Millions*, also published by Atlantic Publishing Company in 2009.

Index

We recently lost our beloved pet "Bear," who was not only
our best and dearest friend but also the "Vice President of
Sunshine" here at Atlantic Publishing. He did not receive
a salary but worked tirelessly 24 hours a day to please
his parents. Bear was a rescue dog that turned around
and showered myself, my wife Sherri, his grandparents
Jean, Bob and Nancy and every person and animal he met
(maybe not rabbits) with friendship and love. He made a
lot of people smile every day.

We wanted you to know that a portion of the profits of this
book will be donated to The Humane Society of
the United States.

–Douglas & Sherri Brown

THE HUMANE SOCIETY
OF THE UNITED STATES ©

The human-animal bond is as old as human history. We cherish our animal companions for their unconditional affection and acceptance. We feel a thrill when we glimpse wild creatures in their natural habitat or in our own backyard.

Unfortunately, the human-animal bond has at times been weakened. Humans have exploited some animal species to the point of extinction.

The Humane Society of the United States makes a difference in the lives of animals here at home and worldwide. The HSUS is dedicated to creating a world where our relationship with animals is guided by compassion. We seek a truly humane society in which animals are respected for their intrinsic value, and where the human-animal bond is strong.

Want to help animals? We have plenty of suggestions. Adopt a pet from a local shelter, join The Humane Society and be a part of our work to help companion animals and wildlife. You will be funding our educational, legislative, investigative and outreach projects in the U.S. and across the globe.

Or perhaps you'd like to make a memorial donation in honor of a pet, friend or relative? You can through our Kindred Spirits program. And if you'd like to contribute in a more structured way, our Planned Giving Office has suggestions about estate planning, annuities, and even gifts of stock that avoid capital gains taxes.

Maybe you have land that you would like to preserve as a lasting habitat for wildlife. Our Wildlife Land Trust can help you. Perhaps the land you want to share is a backyard—that's enough. Our Urban Wildlife Sanctuary Program will show you how to create a habitat for your wild neighbors.

So you see, it's easy to help animals. And The HSUS is here to help.

The Humane Society of the United States
2100 L Street NW
Washington, DC 20037
202-452-1100
www.hsus.org

   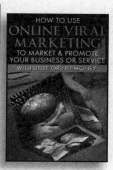